THE
Millionaire Map

THE
Millionaire Map

THE ULTIMATE GUIDE
TO CREATING, ENJOYING, AND
SHARING WEALTH

Jim Stovall

Sound Wisdom
167 Walnut Bottom Road
Shippensburg, PA 17257

For more information on foreign distribution,
call 717-530-2122.
Reach us on the Internet: www.soundwisdom.com

This book and all other Sound Wisdom books are available at bookstores and distributors worldwide.

ISBN 13 TP: 978-1-937879-36-5
ISBN 13 Ebook: 978-1-937879-37-2

For Worldwide Distribution, Printed in the U.S.A.
1 2 3 4 5 6 7 8 9 10 / 17 16 15 14 13

Dedication

This book is dedicated to all of my family, friends, and mentors who have taught, guided, and loved me in both poverty and wealth. Having you in my life has made me rich in every way.

Today

Remember,
God this day unfurled
To everyone
Throughout the world.
Unblemished day,
Bejeweled and pearled—
A gift to you and me.

For each man's a tower
Or just a stone.
Born to climb higher
Or be left alone.
Time is the gift.
Use it with care.
Climb to the heights—
Our dreams flourish there.

From the personal diary of Joye Kanelakos

Contents

CHAPTER ONE

The Millionaire Road Less Traveled

If you want to reach a new destination, you have to travel a new road on your millionaire map.

MY DEAR READER:

You and I are going to be exploring, planning, and launching a special journey within the pages of this book and beyond. Establishing and reaching your millionaire destination is among the most significant things you will ever do in your life.

Money is far from the most important thing in your life, but it affects each and every one of the elements of your life that are vital.

This book may represent your very first effort toward financial success, or you may be among the myriad of people who have made many attempts toward reaching your millionaire status. Regardless of your past experience, this book is different and represents the beginning of your new life and the journey toward your millionaire destination and lifestyle.

This is not a book of academic theories or fantasy get-rich-quick schemes written by an imposter or pretender. I am a self-made millionaire, many times over, who began my financial life at a point of desperation and debt few people have ever experienced.

This book represents wisdom and experience gained from my own journey from poverty to wealth as well as the collective wisdom and experiences of literally thousands of millionaires and billionaires that I have worked with individually and collectively in special events and speaking engagements.

I'm a firm believer that no one with experience ever has to take a back seat to someone with a theory. As you will discover in a later chapter, I have gone to great lengths to verify to you that my own background, experience, and success is real. My staff, my family, and I struggled with the idea of disclosing the origin and amount of my wealth in this book, but I feel it is critical to the success of your journey and part of the extensive commitment I am making to you and your own millionaire journey.

This book is different in another way. After you read the last page of this book and set it aside, our relationship will not be ending. Our journey together will be only just beginning.

You will find many resources, tools, and events through our website, www.TheMillionaireMap.com. I want you to understand and rely on the fact that I am serious about your success. As you launch your journey and move toward your millionaire destination, any time you are encountering challenges, problems, or questions, I can be reached directly via email at Jim@JimStovall.com, or you can call me at 918-627-1000.

When I first became a millionaire after struggling in poverty for years, I thought there could be nothing more exciting than reaching my own millionaire destination; however, over the years since, I have discovered what I hope you will discover after becoming a millionaire yourself which is the fact that it is actually more fun and exciting to help other people join you in reaching their own millionaire destination than it was to achieve your millionaire goals.

I am looking forward to your success and want to share in the celebration with you. As you reach your millionaire milestones, please send me an email and let me know the goals you have reached and what you have gone through and overcome to get there. This will give me the opportunity to congratulate you and send you a gift as my token of celebration and recognition for the effort you have made and the success you have achieved.

Becoming a millionaire is fairly simple, but it's not easy.

I remember when my own millionaire journey began. Like many people reading this book, I began my millionaire journey from a deep, dark hole of debt, despair, depression, and disability. As a blind person, I found myself with no prospects or opportunities as I confronted an overwhelming, growing mountain of debt.

I heard an audio recording made by Dr. Denis Waitley. Little did I know at that time, he would later become my friend, mentor, and write the foreword to my first book. After hearing that recording by Dr. Waitley, I didn't have all the answers or even understand the questions, but I had something I had not had before which was hope.

I contacted Denis Waitley's office and learned that he would be speaking a thousand miles away at an event in two days. My wife Crystal and I loaded up our infamous green Pontiac, which you will learn more about in coming chapters, and we headed for Phoenix, Arizona.

When I filled up the car before leaving town and the service station attendant asked where I was going, I stated with the confidence of the uninitiated and ignorant, "We're going to a meeting in Phoenix."

He laughed heartily and stated for the record, "That car has about as good a chance of getting to Phoenix as it does of getting out of this gas station."

When I got back in the car, Crystal asked if the service station attendant was concerned about our car, and I assured her, "He didn't feel driving this car to Phoenix was any riskier than just driving out of the gas station."

We headed for Phoenix and slept in the car. I had brought my portable tape recorder and was listening to Dr. Waitley's recording over and over as we traveled. I remember him describing "paying the price for success" and "doing the things other people aren't willing to do."

I remember we pulled over to the side of the road about 3:00 a.m. to rest ourselves and the car for a little while. I was thinking about doing the things other people weren't willing to do and I asked Crystal if she saw any other people driving on this road at 3:00 in the morning or sleeping in their decrepit car beside the road.

She assured me that we were alone.

While I questioned the wisdom of our trip, I began to understand for the first time that we were willing to pay the price and do the things other people weren't willing to do.

Please understand that while you are considering the price of success, there is another price you must also consider. I believe that you pay the price of success once and enjoy it from now on. But the price of failure is a debt you will pay every day for the rest of your life.

If you can think the thoughts and dream the dreams of your millionaire destination, you have the spark of hope and the beginning steps of your millionaire journey. I always dreamed that being a millionaire would be a wonderful, magical, and special way to live. I can assure you my millionaire destination and lifestyle is better than I thought it would be, and I know yours will exceed your expectations as well.

It's not simply a matter of the things you will be able to buy and the places you will be able to go. Your millionaire destination represents a whole new world for the people you love, the causes that matter to you, and those who will follow in your footsteps throughout your lifetime and beyond.

CHAPTER TWO

Who Wants to be a Millionaire?

Be sure your map leads to a destination you want to reach.

MANY YEARS AGO, I HEARD a news story about the launch of a new television show. Among my business interests, I own and operate a television network, so a news item about a new program was of particular interest to me.

The news reporter was interviewing Regis Philbin as he was slated to be the host of this new program. I had known of Regis Philbin most of my life. Among my earliest television memories are images of Regis being the sidekick of Joey Bishop on late-night TV. He had his own cable TV interview show for many years when original cable programming was in its infancy. Later, I met Regis Philbin at television industry functions, and I met his co-host, Kathie Lee Gifford, when I appeared on *Good Morning America*.

As the news reporter interviewed Regis about his background in the entertainment industry and the concept of his new program, Regis announced that the show would be called *Who Wants to be a Millionaire?*

The normally-conservative and sober reporter laughed aloud, declaring, "Who wouldn't want to be a millionaire?"

The creators and producers of the game show obviously picked the title *Who Wants to be a Millionaire?* because they felt it would include everyone.

If we are considering the Hollywood, storybook, fairytale image of a millionaire, I would agree that everyone would want to be a millionaire. But if we're thinking about the real work-a-day world where you and I live which includes difficult budget, savings, and investment decisions, as well as career choices and a myriad of business opportunities, the answer to the question, "Who wants to be a millionaire?" may not be so simple.

Obviously, you are reading this book because you have goals, objectives, or just questions that involve the topic of money. Money is probably the most misunderstood concept in our society.

I watched Regis Philbin's *Who Wants to be a Millionaire* show a handful of times but the "Millionaire" show that really captured my attention as a teenager or young adult was a program called *Lifestyles of the Rich and Famous.* On this show, the host, Robin Leach, who is among the most imitated, ridiculed, and satirized TV personalities of all time, took the viewers on a worldwide tour of the very best, most expensive, and most exclusive places in the world. The more outlandish and over-the-top, the better it was on *Lifestyles of the Rich and Famous.*

At the end of each show, I was left with two diverse thoughts and points of view. On one hand, some of the places and things seemed wonderful, and on the other hand, some of the ways people spent their money seemed so absurd that I remember thinking: *I don't care how much money you've got, it's stupid to spend it on something like that.*

Money is a tool that can be used in virtually any way we choose. More than anything else, money represents choices. Money can buy the most useful and beneficial things in the world, or it can purchase frustration and destruction.

By now, you are probably wondering if this book is really going to tell you how to be a millionaire or try to convince you not to be. I can assure you that this book will definitely live up to its title; however, before you set out on a quest to become a millionaire, I want to be sure you understand where you are going, what it means, and what you will need to give up to get there.

We've all had the experience of contemplating a trip through travel videos or resort brochures. It's always sunny, all the people are friendly, and everything is postcard perfect. Travelers returning from some of those destinations might tell us a very different story.

The Internet has given us all the ability to not only review the sales pitch for any travel location but also to see what others who have been there have to say about the destination.

I don't want you to get a good impression or bad impression of being a millionaire. I want you to, instead, have an accurate impression of becoming a millionaire before you begin your journey.

Books, movies, television, myths, and legends have colored our ideas of what it means to become a millionaire. Your first step on your millionaire mission is to get a clear picture of your destination and what it will take to get there.

As a blind person myself, it is embarrassing to admit to you as you are reading a book I have written that when I could read with my eyes, as you are reading the print on the pages of the book you hold in your hands, I don't know that I ever read an entire book, cover to cover. I skimmed enough text books to get through school, but the idea of sitting down and reading an entire book never occurred to me at that time. After losing my sight, I discovered audio books and how to listen to them at high speed. More than two decades after losing my sight, I have experienced the life-changing reality of reading, on average, one book a day for over 20 years. This process has changed my life and has done more to improve my existence as a millionaire and in every other way than virtually anything else.

Several years ago, I read a number of books about mountain climbing. I have never climbed a mountain and probably never will, but I find the concept of identifying a mountain and devising a way to climb it very compelling.

One of the many books I read involved two middle-aged businessmen with virtually no mountaineering experience climbing the tallest peak on each continent within a year. The obstacles they overcame and hardships they endured made an exciting and heroic book.

I remember the account of these businessmen traveling to Antarctica to climb the tallest mountain on that forbidding, frozen continent. After many arduous weeks of travel and preparation, they began climbing toward the peak. As they were approaching a critical point in their climb, a radio message from base camp ordered them to stop until a surveyor's calculation could determine whether or not they were on the right mountain.

This is, obviously, something they would have liked to have known before all the time, effort, and energy had been expended to climb a considerable way up the mountain where they were precariously perched. The calculations eventually confirmed that they were, indeed, on the correct mountain, but the lesson remains that we should double check our destination as well as our route before we begin the journey.

By strict definition, becoming a millionaire does not necessarily mean that you live in a mansion, drive the most expensive cars, and vacation in the most remote or exotic places. Being a millionaire, for the sake of this book, will mean you have a million dollars of net worth or more.

When the term millionaire came into vogue several centuries ago, it represented a vast amount of money which caused the word "millionaire" to take on almost mythical proportions. Today, depending on where you live, a fairly modest home might be worth a million dollars, and people who have worked at a job where their employer provides and contributes to a retirement plan may have well over a million dollars of net worth in their retirement account; therefore, for the sake of the quest you and I will be contemplating and launching within the pages of this book, we will define becoming a millionaire as reaching all of your financial goals.

In our definition of a millionaire, money will not be of prime importance. On the contrary, becoming a millionaire by our definition in this book will mean that you can make all of the decisions you make in your life without money becoming a significant factor. This is a rare condition that very few people ever experience.

For the vast majority of people, the home where you live, the vehicle you drive, the clothes you wear, the school your children attend, the restaurant you frequent and what you eat, how you contribute to the causes and charities that matter to you, and even how you spend the hours of every day of your life are greatly determined by money.

If you have the money you need to have and do all of the things you want in your life, you are financially successful, and you have achieved millionaire status. On the other hand, if you have a billion dollar net worth but there are significant things you want to do in your life that you cannot financially afford, we would have to say you are not a successful millionaire yet by this book's definition.

We are exposed to literally thousands of advertising, promotion, and marketing images every day. Radio, television, the print media, and the Internet constantly feed us a sumptuous smorgasbord of ads for every imaginable type of product and service. This endless string of commercial messages is designed to convince us we are not acceptable as we currently are; however, if we will just pick up the nearest phone, click on an Internet ad or rush to the nearest shopping mall, we can remedy every deficiency in our lives.

Within the definitions we will establish in this book, there is virtually nothing money can buy for you that is either good or bad in and of itself. Unfortunately, the media and societal pressure urge us to buy the right things for the wrong reasons.

Becoming a millionaire is not about convincing everyone else that you are a millionaire. It does not involve any specific possessions or number of zeroes on a bank or brokerage account. Becoming a millionaire is, first and foremost, a matter of living your life on your own terms. This is, quite probably, much more elusive than just becoming a technical millionaire.

Through my books, movies, and speaking events, I have met literally thousands of millionaires. While these people have all achieved a measure of financial success, very few of them are actually living their lives on their own terms.

Many millionaires are more dissatisfied with their lives now than when they lived in poverty. For these people, becoming a millionaire has only given them a glimpse of an endless universe of things they don't have. These unhappy millionaires have bought a ticket into an unwinnable game at a higher level. They have fallen prey to what I call *The Disease of More*.

I'm convinced that anyone reading this book can achieve every financial goal that you have in your life, but you can never reach the level of More.

The poster child for *The Disease of More*, in my mind, would be the Dickens character, Scrooge. The idea of being, doing, and having things was left far behind as Ebenezer Scrooge plunged headlong into a lifelong race to achieve the elusive concept of More.

You can have everything you need and even everything you want, but you can't always have more for its own sake. More doesn't exist. It is a direction but not a destination.

You and I can set out to travel to any city in the world and arrive safely at our destination; however, if we determine to travel east, we can move in that direction, but we will never arrive. As you establish your millionaire destination, you can strive for More as a direction along the way, but More will never be a happy ending.

When people set out to become a millionaire, it is because of one of two motivations. Either there is something they want or something they don't want. In my case, it was the latter.

As a teenager and young adult, I had no goal beyond becoming a professional football player. This was the direction I had planned, and I felt I needed no alternatives or safety net. Then, during a routine physical to play another season of football, I was diagnosed with a condition that would result in my blindness.

My casual research told me, at that time and to this very day, there has never been a blind guy play in the NFL. From time to time, there are a few referees that fall under suspicion, but I am assured there are no blind football players.

Not knowing what else to do, I enrolled in a local university and began pursuing a degree.

I was rapidly losing my sight and found it impossible to read and difficult to get around on my own. A young lady named Crystal was assigned to me to read my textbooks. She did a stellar job then just as she does now, having been my wife for more than 30 years. She graduated first in our degree program, and I graduated second. I've always suspected she may have left a little bit out as she was reading my textbooks to me. I have no evidence of this, but it makes me feel better about coming in second.

As my senior year of college approached, many of the other guys that lived in my dormitory were being recruited by corporate headhunters for great jobs after graduation. Suffice it to say, there was no line of recruiters at my door to hire the washed-up, former football-playing, soon-to-be blind guy.

I called my father who had worked in the administration of a nonprofit organization for many years. I told him my latest bright idea involving not getting a job after graduation but starting my own business. He told me to stop by his office the next afternoon, and he would give me something.

Thinking he was probably going to give me some money to start my mythical business, I arrived early the next day. He immediately burst my bubble by telling me, "I'm not going to give you any money, but I am going to provide you with two things."

I couldn't imagine what he was going to give me that could be worth anything compared to the startup capital I was hoping for. He explained, "First, I'm going to give you the certain knowledge that if you ever earn anything in this world, you got it on your own. And, second, since I have no experience as an entrepreneur, I'm going to introduce you to a self-made millionaire."

This began my learning experience with Lee Braxton. I have received an inordinate amount of undue praise from people from all around the world simply for disseminating wisdom I got from Lee Braxton in the form of books, movies, television, syndicated columns, and speeches.

After graduation, I began my business career, and Crystal and I were married. To say that money was tight would be the biggest understatement since Noah said, "It looks like rain."

Every week, Crystal and I would go together to the grocery store. She had a calculator with her, and I had all the money we had in the world in my pocket. As we picked out what we would eat for the coming week, Crystal entered the prices into the calculator until the grand total reached the amount I had in my pocket.

One fateful day in the grocery store, somehow we misfigured, and we had more groceries in our cart than we had money. Right there in front of friends, neighbors, and a condescending checkout girl, Crystal had to go and put a loaf of bread back on the shelf. That instant, my millionaire quest began. I had no idea what it would take to become financially successful or a millionaire; I simply knew I never wanted to experience that feeling again.

Once you can feel that kind of passion or emotion for something you want or don't want, your millionaire status is simply a matter of time.

Before we fill in your millionaire map and you start your journey, be sure that you emotionally own your destination. This is to say that I had to take ownership of that feeling and those emotions connected to that single loaf of bread those many years ago in the grocery store. You can't chase someone else's dream or follow their millionaire map.

I had a friend who began his entrepreneurial millionaire quest at about the same time I did. My friend was a few years older than me, and we stayed in regular contact, supporting one another through our trials and tribulations. After several years of struggling, he called me and said, "I've decided to let go of this millionaire thing and go a different direction."

He explained that because of a divorce and instantly becoming a single dad, his former goal of becoming a millionaire had been replaced by the desire to go to every one of his kids' ballgames, scouting events, and school programs. He got a manufacturing job and worked 10 hours a day, Monday through Thursday, so he would have a three-day weekend every week.

My friend got season tickets to all of the pro football games in his area, and he never missed the opening day of fishing season or hunting season for many years. His kids grew up to be model citizens and when I calculate the love and respect everyone in that family has for one another, I count my friend among the most successful and wealthy people I know.

Ironically, not too long ago, my friend and I were fishing at a very scenic lake together. We had not talked about business or finance for many years, silently agreeing to respect the decisions we each had made for our own lives and the corresponding success we have each enjoyed.

As we were fishing, out of the blue he inquired, "Can I ask you a financial question?"

I assured him I would help in any way I could, and he explained that even though 24 years earlier he had released his goal of being a millionaire, every year since he had invested diligently in his company's retirement plan, and now in his late 50s, he was enjoying a wonderful family, a great life, and he is finally a millionaire.

While the rest of this book will be dedicated to helping you become a millionaire, be sure that while you're pursuing the things that money will buy that you don't miss the things in life that money won't buy.

CHAPTER THREE

The Map Maker

Never accept a map from someone
who hasn't been where you want to go.

WE LIVE IN A WORLD that, when it's all said and done, there's a lot said and very little done.

Throughout recorded history, various periods of time have become known for their art, architecture, or public persona. Hence, we have the Golden Age, the Renaissance, the Industrial Revolution, etc. Hundreds of years from now, the period in which you and I live might well become known as the Age of Hype.

Everything is enhanced, new and improved, miraculous, and every other conceivable adjective which is designed to encourage you and me to buy into a marketing presentation instead of reality. Elements of human conduct that generations ago used to be black and white, take on various shades of gray. Whether it's our political leaders, a business icon, or the clergy, messages are synthesized, spun, and inflated until they are barely recognizable. The phrase "Fake it until you make it" which used to be a blatant insult to people of our parents' or grandparents' generation is now considered to be a sound business strategy.

I am a firm believer that everyone's personal finances and net worth are a private matter of concern only to them, their family, or their organization. Right up until the point where they are asking you or me to make a time or money decision based on their advice, expertise, or experience.

I have written 20 books. Several of them have been made into major motion pictures with others in production. I have written hundreds of columns, syndicated in newspapers, magazines, and online publications around the world, read by millions of people each week. With the writing of this *Millionaire Map* book, I am entering a slightly new realm.

My previous books have advised people on how to set their goals, how to live their lives, how to work and deal with others, and even how to save and invest their money; but when you begin telling people how to become a millionaire, I believe you step up to a new level of accountability and scrutiny. The best advice I have ever received on the subject of advice is quite simply, "Never take advice from anyone who doesn't have what you want." This would include fat diet doctors, out-of-shape workout trainers, lawyers who are currently incarcerated, disheveled tailors, and anyone else who doesn't walk the proverbial talk.

As you and I explored in Chapter One, there is absolutely nothing wrong with deciding not to be a millionaire or not to make wealth a priority in your life. Millions of people with average incomes and modest net worths live fulfilling, meaningful, and significant lives.

Unless there's something you want to do, have, or give that requires millions of dollars, being a millionaire doesn't really qualify you to do anything other than tell other people how to become millionaires.

For many years, I have been fortunate to be among the highest-paid arena and corporate speakers in the world. I have met literally hundreds of professional speakers, trainers, and seminar leaders. I have been a bestselling author with millions of books in print. Each of my books, including this one, provides my phone number: 918-627-1000. With millions of people around the world having my phone number, you might imagine how many people call me. I return each of these calls, and if you find this hard to believe, please feel free to join the ever-growing group of people who try it out.

One of the most prevalent groups of people who regularly call me is aspiring or fledgling authors, speakers, coaches, consultants, or seminar leaders. I have literally spoken to hundreds of individuals who want to make a living telling other people how to be successful, run a business, or create wealth. The only problem is that most of these people have never done what they purport to tell others how to do.

Before you read anyone's book, listen to their speech, take their course, or pay for their advice, be sure that they have what you want. Anyone who is not a millionaire is not a good guide to help you become a millionaire. Either they don't know how to get there, or it's not a priority in their life. In either case, it makes them a poor person for you to follow on your quest to become a millionaire.

There is probably no one reading these pages that has ever been more broke, scared, or depressed than I have been. I hasten to say that, from a global perspective, most of us reading this book are already rich. When I refer to my own poverty, I'm speaking of First World poor and not Third World poor. Later in this book, we will discuss what you and I can do to make a difference for people who are truly less fortunate.

I was born in America, received a positive and nurturing upbringing, and got a college education. For these things and many others, I recognize that I am truly blessed. On the other hand, I know what it's like to owe more money than you can imagine without the current ability to even pay the interest. I know what it's like to go months at a time never missing a payment but always having less than $1,000 in the checking account. I know what it's like to scramble for the most basic elements of food, clothing, and shelter. I know the feeling of hearing a strange noise coming from the car engine, the refrigerator, or the hot water heater that signals not a looming repair or an inconvenience but an all-out crisis. I have never inherited any money, won the lottery, or done anything else that everyone reading this book couldn't do.

Well into my adulthood, I had a net worth of zero or, like many Americans, less than zero. At this writing, I have joined the fraction of one percent of people who are deca-millionaires, people who have in excess of $10 million. I realize that identifying myself with the top one percent of wealth holders makes me unpopular in some circles. I have found that millionaires comprise the only criticized group of people that everyone seems to want to join.

As I mentioned at the outset of this chapter, we live in a world where there is much said and little done. It's easy for anyone to make the kinds of statements I have just made, and many self-appointed experts who don't have the price of bus fare constantly make similar claims. For this reason, I have made arrangements with the investment banking firm that I have worked with for two decades. They have independently reviewed and are prepared to verify these statements and my net worth to you. You can review this verification and contact them via www.TheMillionaire Map.com.

I make these claims and verifications for no self-serving reasons. In fact, among the countless words I have written over the years, this chapter deals with one of the hardest topics about which I have ever written, but I feel it is so critical to your success I have undertaken to qualify myself as someone whose advice, experience, and expertise you can judge in light of my millionaire status.

Through my other books and particularly a novel I wrote entitled *The Ultimate Gift* which was subsequently made into a movie by 20ᵗʰ Century Fox, I have been invited to speak at a number of family gatherings of billionaires. These billionaire families invite me to speak to their second and third generations in order to deal with issues of legacy, philanthropy, and other pertinent topics you and I will explore through the ensuing chapters.

In meeting, working with, and becoming friends with a number of these billionaires, I can assure you they live, move, and have their being in a different realm than most people you will ever meet. I readily admit I am not a billionaire, and if this is a status you seek, you will want to look to one of them for advice and guidance once you have already become a multimillionaire.

Lest you think I am committing far too much effort and energy toward this topic of authenticity and verifiability, recently I have perused a number of investment, business opportunity, and wealth seminar ads, all of which purport to make you wealthy. After responding to dozens of these promotional ads, I was unable to find even one millionaire among the people selling the products and services or clients they have served.

In preparation for writing this book, I have gone to a number of financial and wealth seminars over the past few years. Recently, I attended an event put on at a local hotel which claimed to be able to show you how to "become rich through real estate." The event bore the name of a well-known author and speaker whom I have worked with in the past. The meeting room was very nice, and the staff was very polite and professional. After a somewhat sketchy presentation with virtually no concrete facts or evidence to back up their claims, I was shocked when dozens of people rushed to purchase a training package which cost several hundred dollars. My fellow attendees at that event did not seem to be the kind of people who could just throw hundreds of dollars out the window. Additionally, this training program involved a three-day course.

Remember, you can lose your money and make more, but you can never replace your time. It's important to always be investing your time in the right way because when you're wasting time, you're not just standing still. You're failing to move in the direction you should be traveling.

After this particular real estate wealth event, I talked to several of the staff members who had conducted the meeting. I was shocked to learn that not only were they not wealthy real estate investors, but they had not even taken the course and further revealed that they could not afford to stay in the nice hotel where the meeting was held, and they hoped they had enough gas money to get to the next town.

I believe, had those eager people who invested their time and money in that program simply known the truth about those individuals who were promoting the training course, the outcome would have been much different. There is nothing wrong with not having enough money to stay in a nice hotel or even being concerned about having enough gas money to get to the next town. I will readily admit to having experienced both conditions; however, it becomes relevant, pertinent, and vital if that is the status of someone who is advising you on how to become a millionaire.

My first millionaire mentor was a gentleman named Lee Braxton. I met Mr. Braxton through my father as I described earlier. Mr. Braxton served on the board of a nonprofit organization where my father worked.

Lee Braxton never attended graduate school and never received an MBA, a finance degree, or any other credential that you would recognize. In fact, he had a third-grade education. He did not come from a wealthy family, and he made his fortune during the Great Depression.

Mr. Braxton had no educational, political, or professional standing that most people would recognize as qualifying him to be my mentor. In fact, the only qualification he had to mentor me was the fact that he was a self-made multimillionaire. That was the only qualification he had and the only one I needed.

As we began our mentoring relationship, he made it very clear I was going to have to do all the work, and there would be a lot of reading involved. I had a million questions on how to get a lot of money, and he simply handed me a book and said, "Read this then come back, and we'll discuss it." I continued to ask questions, and he just smiled and nodded toward the book in my hands and walked away.

The book Mr. Braxton gave me was *Think and Grow Rich* by Napoleon Hill. One of the handful of characteristics that self-made millionaires have in common is the fact that they read many more books than the general public. Surveys of self-made millionaires and Fortune 500 CEOs show that among the handful of books most often read by these top achievers is Napoleon Hill's *Think and Grow Rich*. I didn't know then that Lee Braxton had been a personal friend of Napoleon Hill, and Mr. Braxton actually gave the eulogy at Napoleon Hill's funeral. Today, among my most prized possessions is a 50-year-old copy of *Think and Grow Rich* autographed by Napoleon Hill, given to me by Don Green who runs the Napoleon Hill Foundation.

In the last few years, I have had the privilege of working with the Napoleon Hill Foundation to provide endorsements and commentaries on some of Napoleon Hill's never-before-released teachings.

Mr. Braxton taught me the power of getting the right mentors in my life. He told me eventually I would have my own team of people helping me to the top, but at that time, he made it clear that the only way I was going to get exposure to top people's wisdom and experience was through their books.

The greatest minds that the world has ever known, including those who will help you become a millionaire, are available to you any time through the pages of books. As you build your own dream team of mentors—in person as well as virtually through their books, DVDs, and audio recordings—always remember that you will have to seek out and pursue great mentors while the charlatans, frauds, and want-to-bes will aggressively pursue you.

When I look at my own millionaire quest in general or building any of my business interests specifically, I start by building my own dream team. I always ask myself, "Who are the 10 people who have been where I want to go and can tell me how to get there?" You should never limit this list to the people you have access to or know how to contact. Simply make your dream team list of the best people you can think of, whether you believe you can connect with them or not.

As we go through the chapters that will lead you toward your millionaire status, you will find that I am a big believer in "Never get the question of 'How you are going to do it?' mixed up with the question of 'What are you going to do?'"

When I began my business in the television and movie industry, I had no background, training, or experience, I knew no one in the field, and I lived in Tulsa, Oklahoma, which is not exactly the entertainment capital of the world.

My first venture, the Narrative Television Network, is a company that makes movies and television accessible for millions of blind people like me. I realized that this was quite a departure from anything that had ever been done in the industry, so as I started making my dream team list of people who could get me from where I was to where I wanted to be, I thought of the biggest innovators or trend-setters in the business. The first name that popped into my mind was Ted Turner.

Through 24-hour news, the superstation concept, and a number of specialty networks, Mr. Turner changed the industry. I had never met Ted Turner, I didn't know anyone who had met Ted Turner, and I didn't have a clue how to get in touch with him; but I put him on my dream team list.

By calling directory assistance in Atlanta, Georgia, I got a phone number for Turner Broadcasting. I called the number and asked for a mailing address. Then I sat down and wrote a one-page letter describing to Ted Turner my hopes, goals, and dreams of making movies and television accessible to blind people.

It wasn't long until Mr. Turner contacted me and helped me locate programming, contact stations, and gave me the encouragement and advice I needed to begin the journey. As absurd as it seems to me now, it was just that simple.

Someone long before me declared the wisdom, "You have not because you ask not."

I have been ignored and turned down many times, but in addition to Mr. Turner, my mentors in the TV and movie industry have included Steve Allen, Frank Sinatra, Katharine Hepburn, Jimmy Stewart, and many others. In the finance and wealth arena, my mentors include Steve

Forbes, Donald Trump, Dr. Denis Waitley, Paul Harvey, legendary Coach John Wooden, and a significant group of other people who willingly advised, mentored, and encouraged a struggling young blind guy with nothing more than a big dream.

As you read these words, you may feel as I did when I got started along the road to becoming a millionaire. I felt I had absolutely nothing and, therefore, I had nothing to lose. This wasn't true for me, and it isn't true for you. What I had then and what, hopefully, you have now, is the hope, desire, and dream to create enough value in the world so that you can become wealthy.

My friend and mentor in the speaking and writing industry, Zig Ziglar, said it best. "You can have everything you want if you will just help enough other people get what they want."

You must protect your attitude, your ambition, and your dream. There are countless scams, frauds, and deceptive deals that will divert you and leave you lying in the ditch along the road to your millionaire destination.

It's not hard to get great advice, direction, and mentoring if you can remove all of the noise coming from the hucksters and thieves clamoring for your time and money. My grandfather, who was a great gardener, told me that all you need to do to have little tiny seeds grow into big healthy plants is keep everything away from them that wants to destroy them. I know I seem rather harsh and judgmental with regard to people who want to take your time and money purporting to give you something you don't have.

My vehemence comes from the fact that they're not just stealing your time and money. They're stealing your dream.

Anything worth your time and money as you pursue your wealth goals is worthy of checking out and verifying. Legitimate people will welcome your inquiries and due diligence. The frauds, hype artists, and thieves will scatter like roaches when you turn the light on to examine the reality of their claims, their experience, and their expertise.

People who have really succeeded will prove to be surprisingly open and available to you as you pursue your destiny along the route of your Millionaire Map; but remember, they won't seek you out. You have to approach them. You won't find these millionaire mentors on late night cable TV or in a slick advertisement. Like gold, diamonds, and all treasures on earth, great mentors have to be sought out and uncovered.

When you reach your millionaire goals, as you inevitably will, you will realize that you are standing on the shoulders of giants. These are the men and women who have gone before you who gladly invest their time and experience in your dreams. When you reach your destination, the only thing you can do to repay them is what I have sought to do for many years, which is to believe in the dreams of others and help them join you in living out a millionaire destiny.

CHAPTER FOUR

The Most Important Point on the Map

You can't figure out where you're going or how to get there until you know where you are.

IN THE BEGINNING OF THIS book, we explored whether or not you really want to be a millionaire. Even though we now understand it's perfectly acceptable not to pursue becoming a millionaire, I will assume that, since you have reached Chapter Four, achieving millionaire status is still an important part of your life.

In Chapter Three, we introduced the concept of understanding all the fakes, frauds, and scam artists who are much more interested in getting their hands on the money you've got instead of helping you accumulate the money you want.

Now, we will establish one of the most important foundations you will need on your journey to your financial goals.

A millionaire map or any map can be the most critical element of getting from where you are to where you want to be, but the best organized and most detailed map in the world is useless unless you know one thing. Before you can establish your destination or even your route to get there, you must know exactly where you are today.

People seem to understand and accept this concept in every area of life except for their finances. You can go into any mall in America, and they will have detailed diagrams of the locations of all the stores. These diagrams will be strategically located throughout the mall near the entrances, exits, elevators, and stairways. Each of the diagrams is likely to look exactly like all the others regardless of its location within the mall. The only variable will be one minute point on the diagram with a brief notation stating, "You are here." That minute point on the diagram is the key to getting from where you are to where you want to be.

We are all familiar with the global positioning technology in vehicles and phones that make navigating in the 21st century simple compared to anything that our ancestors experienced as they tried to find their way from where they were to where they wanted to be. I find it amazing that highways, streets, intersections, and house numbers for virtually any location in the world have been entered into centralized databases that are accessed by these global positioning devices.

The work involved in compiling all of this information and data boggles my mind, but what made our travel simple was not the mass of data and information compiled. It was the fact that, for the first time ever, technology made it possible for a satellite orbiting in space to determine exactly our current location. Once you know your current location, you can begin an organized, systematic journey toward anywhere you want to go.

Like many Americans of my generation, I find myself in a constant diet and exercise battle to lose weight and get in better physical condition. As a former Olympic weightlifter, I spent a lot of my early years working out and training more than most people could ever imagine, followed by eating more than most people could ever imagine. While I don't work out like I used to, if I don't watch myself carefully, I can still eat like an Olympic weightlifter.

When I consult my doctor or a trainer regarding my latest diet and exercise plan, the first thing they invariably want to do is put me on a scale and weigh me. I do not want to be weighed as I know it will reveal a number I'm not comfortable with which is the very condition that triggered my consultation in the first place.

My university degree is in Psychology / Sociology, so I have some understanding of why human beings in general, and I specifically, find certain numbers to be uncomfortable. On the other hand, as someone who spends most of my professional life delivering messages through books, movies, TV, syndicated columns, and speeches regarding how people can reach their goals, I know it is vital to establish a baseline and understand your current position.

Although I find the 10 Commandments to be plenty to think about and deal with in my daily life, several years ago I established a concept I call Stovall's 11th Commandment. This commandment states emphatically, "Thou shall not kid thyself."

One of the other commandments vital in this discussion states, "Thou shall not lie." This is important as I believe the only real lies humans deal with are the lies they tell themselves. Then they communicate this lie with everyone else. If you will lie to yourself, you will lie to anyone, so it's important we begin with the absolute, totally accurate, unvarnished truth.

My friend and mentor, Dr. Robert Schuler, without whose influence I never would have written my first book much less this one which is my twentieth book, often says, "Starting is halfway there."

When I began writing this book, I dictated the first sentence you read in Chapter One. I realize, technically from a mathematical perspective, that first sentence does not represent half of this book, but I also understand, as a lifelong student of human behavior and success, that if you gathered up all the people in the world who say they want to write a book and you then examine the ones who have actually written the first sentence, you will find that, indeed, starting the project puts you far ahead of much more than half the people.

The effort and energy it takes to lose weight, get in shape, graduate from college, drive across the country, or become a millionaire doesn't begin when you commence your journey. It begins when you start your plan.

Planning is the most vital part of any operation. I realize some people suffer from analysis paralysis and never get out of the planning stage.

General George Patton was fond of saying, "A good plan violently executed today is better than a perfect plan next week."

As you continue through this book, you will be able to establish your plan and begin your journey. Neither your plan nor your journey will be perfect, and they will always be a work in progress, but you've got to start somewhere, and that process begins here and now.

You will never become a millionaire—regardless of external plans, opportunities, or connections—unless you figure out exactly where you are today. I realize this is a painful process. If you were pleased with your current financial condition, you would not have wasted your money buying nor your time reading this book.

The most important number you will ever calculate and reveal in your financial quest is your current net worth. For the majority of people reading this book, that number will begin with a minus sign.

Recently, I was enjoying a PBS special featuring one of our country's leading financial experts. The topic of the show was surrounding how to become a successful investor and manage your money. There was a studio audience of approximately 100 people representing a diverse population.

I will never forget the host asking everyone to stand up who did not have credit card debt, student loan debt, automobile loans, or any other consumer debt. I was really shocked when only a handful of people in that television audience stood up. The majority of people who had come to learn from one of the most recognized financial experts in the entire world how they should invest their money, in reality, had no money to invest. If this is you, it's okay because we've got to start somewhere, and the place to start is here, and the time is now.

Most people not only have no money, they don't even know how far in debt they really are. They assume, "If I can't pay these bills, why should I open them up, look at them, and calculate the total amount of money I can't pay." I understand this emotion and can even accept it if you were going to stay where you are today. But if you're going to become a millionaire and utilize the millionaire map, we've got to find the financial point that signifies, "You are here."

I can remember being in debt and owing more money than I could imagine. It was in the 1980s, and interest rates were approaching 20 percent. As I was trying to ignore my mounting debt and financial problems, the lead story on every news broadcast seemed to be the latest new record-breaking high interest rate. I didn't want to know how much I owed or how much the interest would be on that amount of money because I didn't have either the principle or the interest.

I was never willing to endure the pain of revealing the extent of my financial obesity until that fateful day in the grocery store when I didn't have enough money to buy a loaf of bread. That one loaf of bread has become worth many millions of dollars to me. It didn't make me any money directly, but it caused me to figure out where I was and where I didn't want to be ever again.

Once you have added up everything you owe and subtracted everything you own, you can find out how far in the hole you are. If you are experiencing better financial health than most people, you may own more than you owe which means you will be starting from a number that begins with a plus sign. If you owe more than you own, it may be painful to admit it to yourself, but I believe you are well along the path to your financial destination simply by virtue of figuring out where you are.

If you are in a financial hole represented by your current debt and you want to build a financial skyscraper of a future, the first thing you've got to do is stop digging the hole. If you want to go up financially, you've got to stop going down first. While this might seem overly simplistic, it is a financial concept that our elected officials in Washington, DC, don't seem to be able to grasp. You cannot borrow and spend your way to becoming a millionaire. At some point you're going to have to spend less than you earn, and make your money work as hard for you as you work for it.

Much of the wealth you are seeking is already passing through your hands and your checkbook each month. The average American will earn well over a million dollars in their lifetime. Financially, they are like someone trying to fill a bathtub while leaving the drain open. You can create Niagara Falls without accumulating any water if you drain it off faster than you get it.

I remember when Crystal and I sat down and did the painful calculation I am asking you to do. We added up all our debts, which was not an insignificant task, and then we added up all of our assets and income, which was disturbingly simple. The resulting net worth number had six figures and had a minus sign in front of it. As I sat and contemplated my financial goals and dreams in light of that immense negative number, I was discouraged; and when I considered that number growing by 20 percent each year via the high interest rates, I was overwhelmed.

As a multimillionaire today, I am amazed by a financial concept known as compounding. I consider compounding to be the 8th Wonder of the World. Money begets more money at an unbelievable rate once you apply compounding. It's like a snowball rolling over and over as it goes downhill. Each revolution, it picks up more snow, making it grow even bigger as it rolls along.

Unfortunately, I was first exposed to the power of compounding from the perspective of debt, not income and growth. I not only had to stop digging my hole deeper. I had to claw my way out of the hole while paying a huge interest load for the privilege of being in the hole in the first place.

I remember at that time reading every book and attending every financial seminar I could find. I studied and received my financial license and even had a practice as an investment broker for several years. I remember going to my first financial seminar where a self-proclaimed expert was going to show everyone assembled "How to become a successful investor."

I was excited when I heard about the event and got there early as I felt great anticipation of learning how to handle money successfully so I could finally get out of debt and start my process of wealth building. I will never forget the feeling as the seminar leader strode to the front of the room. He was a distinguished middle-aged man whose suit probably cost more than our car. He greeted everyone and confidently began his presentation with a line I will never forget. He wrote a number on the board as he said, "Let's assume you start with $100,000."

He proceeded to tell everyone else how to invest their $100,000, but I was unable to process or even hear anything else he said for the rest of the evening as I began to understand the reality of the fact that before I could even contemplate the finish line, I had to do a lot of work to get to the starting line.

We will discuss many other numbers in the course of this book. All of them are helpful, but your current net worth is vital. As you get closer and closer to your financial goals, you will find it easier and more pleasant to monitor your net worth in much the same way that as I approach my ideal weight I am more comfortable getting on the scales.

I can remember each of the milestones along the way from poverty to wealth. While reaching the $1 million and the $10 million level were cause for celebration, the most exciting milestone of my journey was earning the dollar that represented my negative number becoming zero and then triumphantly becoming $1.

If you find yourself among the growing group of people who will be beginning to build your millionaire skyscraper from somewhere below ground due to your existing debt, there are several concepts which may be helpful.

After you determine the exact dollar amount of the debt you have and commit to stop digging by not borrowing more money, you have to take control of your debt. Just as you went through the painful process of determining the exact number that represents your negative net worth, you must list each of your debts including the amount you owe, the interest rate, and the regular payment. Not only may you find the amount of your debt disturbing, the monthly payments, when added up, may seem daunting as well.

Once you have quantified the amount of your debt, the interest rates, and payments, you must calculate your monthly income minus the cost of your absolute necessities. The amount of your income minus the cost of necessary food, clothing, and shelter will leave you with an amount of money you can utilize each month to pay down your debt.

There are some financial experts who advocate you pay the minimum payments on all debt and commit the excess amount of money you have every month toward the debt with the highest interest rates. This strategy makes the most financial sense as you are eliminating the creditors who cost you the most, first.

Other financial experts suggest you should pay extra on all of your debts or pay the extra on the debt with the smallest principle amount. These methods, while not as mathematically efficient, may provide some psychological benefits as you struggle your way out of the hole your debt has created.

You can shorten the time it will take to get out of your debt hole by focusing on the income side of your equation as well. It's never fun to work overtime or take on a part-time job to pay for mistakes you have made in the past, but if you're going to build your future by letting your money work for you so you can enjoy life in an uncommon way, you may have to do uncommon things to get started.

Just like any detailed roadmap, your millionaire map will offer several routes, any of which will take you to your destination if you remain resolute and committed.

Financial experts disagree on the concept of good debt vs. bad debt. For the sake of your millionaire map and the quest you are beginning, suffice it to say that all consumer debt—including credit cards, department store charges, and unsecured bank loans—should be eliminated forever.

I have interviewed many hundreds of millionaires and billionaires. They have all achieved their financial goals via different routes, but I have never met a millionaire who told me that they borrowed their way to prosperity.

Getting out of the debt hole will enable you to start devoting all of your income to wealth building and will allow you to get that 8th Wonder of the World—compounding—working for you.

After eliminating your debt, there is one more simple but incredible financial concept that will improve the quality of your life as you undertake your quest toward becoming a millionaire. An emergency fund representing from a few months up to one year's worth of your income will change your life.

As I have described earlier, I lived for years in the frustrating, frantic financial dilemma of robbing Peter to pay Paul while putting out fires on a regular basis. While I have grown to understand the value of my experience of not having enough money for a loaf of bread, that feeling is a horrible way to live on an ongoing basis. An emergency fund will take away those nagging distractions represented by the leaky roof, noisy car muffler, or just one loaf of bread more than you calculated.

If you are going to focus your effort and energy on slaying million-dollar financial dragons, you've got to get the minor annoying financial fleas out of your life. Your focus and energy toward your millionaire goals can be derailed by the annoying distraction of a $50 or $100 problem that is a regular occurrence in modern-day life.

In order to climb to the mountain top and live at the financial peak, you've got to crawl out of the valley of debt where you find yourself and avoid the constant annoying financial pitfalls that want to drag you back into that dark and depressing financial hole where you started.

CHAPTER FIVE

Your Millionaire Map Destination

A good map will take you anywhere you want to go, but you have to decide.

IN THE LAST CHAPTER, YOU dealt with the arduous task of soberly gazing into your proverbial financial mirror to determine the exact dollar amount, either positive or negative, you currently have which will signal from where you will begin your millionaire journey.

I have the privilege of speaking to millions of people in corporate and arena events. In each of these speeches, I want to make sure that everyone in my audience knows, just as I want you to know, that you change your life when you change your mind, you have the right to choose, and you are one quality decision away from anything you want. This sentiment applies nowhere more than to your quest of becoming a millionaire and living out all of your goals that are affected by money.

During the process of compiling and quantifying your debts and assets, you likely fell into a trap that catches most people who are undertaking a realistic assessment of their finances. As you reviewed all of your debts or the assets that are not as significant as you had hoped, you may have started to play the blame game. In the blame game, you can look at every debt, every failure, and every wasted opportunity and attach that result to a person or circumstance in your past.

If I were there in your home, office, or at your kitchen table as you were reviewing all of your debts and assets to establish your starting point, you would have probably declared emphatically, much as I did, "It's not my fault because that person or this thing or the other circumstance...." It is critical that you understand that if you are ever to take ownership of your millionaire lifestyle and achieve your millionaire status, you've got to take ownership and lay claim to all of the mistakes, missed opportunities, lackadaisical performance, and lack of focus that has brought you to this place at this time.

As I stated earlier, we each have one true and lasting right in this world and that is the right to choose. We are where we are because of the choices we have made in the past, and only when we accept our past decisions and our resulting position can we then use the same right to choose and exercise it toward becoming a multimillionaire or anything else we want in this life. Please understand I realize that bad things happen to good people, and they often take a toll in our financial lives.

One of the most difficult things about being a blind person is the fact that no one else holds any expectations for you. If I wanted to be a depressed, impoverished slob living off of a government check, I meet all of the qualifications, and no one would say much about it.

I realize you and your family have faced many challenges that, combined together, have put you where you are today; but for every person defeated by blindness, divorce, bankruptcy, or disaster, I will show you someone else who has lived through the same circumstances but has decided to use their current condition as a springboard to their destiny.

Since, in the last chapter, I forced you to get in touch with the mature, adult part of your personality, at this point, I'm going to ask you to focus on your inner child. Now that you know where you will be starting your journey on your millionaire map, next we will identify and locate your destination. Then we will be able to plot a course between the two, and your journey begins.

Selecting your financial goals and millionaire destination is not as easy as it might seem. If you have a two-week vacation approaching, and I ask you the simple question, "Where do you want to go?" you will hear my simple question with your ears, but your mind will translate it to say, "Can I afford to take a trip, how much money do we have to spend, and where can we go with that?"

Most people in the world today haven't considered any significant question for years without processing it through the filter of time and money. I know this is a book about money, but it's impossible to eliminate the discussion of time from the process since the vast majority of the population trades the majority of their time for someone else's money. They invest their days doing work they don't enjoy, for people they don't respect, to earn an income that is not sufficient to take care of those they love in the way they would choose, much less enable them to reach every one of their millionaire financial goals.

Traveling from poverty to becoming a multimillionaire, there have been many fun, pleasant, and significant purchases and acquisitions along the way. While houses, cars, trips, and all manner of luxury items are wonderful to a certain extent, in my world as I evaluate my assets, the number one thing that my money has enabled me to buy is my time. You can earn your money, lose it, and earn more to replace it but no one can give you back last week, last month, or last year.

If, during the course of this exploration of becoming a millionaire, you determine you do not want to get rich and live as a wealthy person, this is fine. I would not argue with you or try to convince you otherwise. It is not important to me that money becomes a priority in your life; however, it is important to me that you begin to see the time you have been given as a treasure. Be careful how you spend it, and don't ever let anyone steal it.

As children, we had the ability to play make-believe and create real environments and circumstances in our own minds.

I was traveling on a commercial airline recently to one of my speaking engagements. One of the few great things about being a blind person is the fact that you get to pre-board the jet with other disabled individuals or those traveling with small children.

On this particular flight, we followed my normal pattern which involves my accompanying colleague and me getting on the plane first and finding our seats in the first non-bulkhead row of first class. As we sat down, I heard a family approaching down the aisle with several young children. An excited young man of approximately five years of age plopped into the first class seat across the aisle from me and began putting on his seatbelt. His mother said, "Brian, we have to sit in row 28."

At that moment, without being disrespectful or even difficult, young Brian asked the question that is the basis of your and my millionaire quest. He inquired, "Mom, why don't we just sit here in first class?"

While there's nothing magic about sitting in first class, I can virtually guarantee you that if you try it, you'll never want to spend a lot of time in coach; however, it may or may not be important to Brian's mother to travel first class, but I'm quite certain there are other priorities that affect her family's lives on a daily basis that she has never considered.

For the next few moments, I want you to join my young traveling friend, Brian, in considering the world you live in without the constraints of time and money that you have put on every element of your life. No one wants a million pieces of wrinkled paper with pictures of dead presidents on them. Having a million dollars or many millions of dollars means absolutely nothing unless it does things for you, or the people you care about, or the world in ways that you find significant.

I'm going to ask you to pick anything you want from the menu of life without letting your eyes wander across the page to the price column. Remember, a big dream doesn't cost any more than a little one, and it's quite often easier to identify with.

Several years ago, I wrote a novel entitled *The Lamp*. It was subsequently made into a major motion picture starring Academy Award-winner Louis Gossett Jr. As in each of the movies that have been made from my novels, I made a brief cameo appearance playing the limo driver. Something has always just made sense to me about having a blind guy drive the limousine.

If you watch *The Lamp* movie, it will appear as if I am driving the limousine through midtown Manhattan in order to drop my passenger, Jason London, off at the Forbes Building. Movie production is magic, and I want to assure you that no New York pedestrians or motorists were injured during the filming of *The Lamp* movie.

In addition to my cameo, I asked several friends who are multimillionaire business colleagues to make brief cameo appearances portraying themselves in the movie. You may enjoy seeing Steve Forbes, Paula Marshall, and Harland Stonecipher in their individual movie debuts.

My friends were intrigued with the story of *The Lamp* book and movie for the same reason that the concept captured me as I was writing *The Lamp*. In the story, a young couple faces unimaginable adversity in their personal and professional lives. Then, through a set of seemingly random happenings, they come into possession of a worthless old oil lamp that no one wanted to buy at a neighborhood garage sale. At the couple's point of utter crisis, the worthless lamp produces a genie. The genie, masterfully played in the film by Lou Gossett, explains to the couple, "You can have anything you want in life, without exception, as long as it's not something you can get on your own, and it doesn't adversely affect anyone else's life."

While it would seem to be a joyous, over-the-moon, lottery-winning moment, the couple struggles to come up with three simple wishes, and in the course of their combined soul searching, it is revealed to them that their every wish was available to them all along.

I won't spoil any more of the plot for you, in case you and your family want to catch *The Lamp*, but if you do get the DVD, one of the menu selections is the success interview special features. I sat down with my multimillionaire business colleague friends to discuss money, success, and life. I believe you will find their comments both revealing and constructive.

One of the most amazing things I have discovered through the process of meeting many millionaires and becoming one myself is the fact that millionaires rarely focus on money. One of the myths we will talk about in a later chapter would have you believe that millionaires are obsessed with money. In reality, I find that people who are in debt and living paycheck to paycheck are far more financially obsessed than millionaires.

Millionaires have a tendency to focus on people, service, creativity, and producing value. Their money is only important to them to the extent that it buys things or experiences they want for themselves or to share with others. This change in mindset is important and will not become possible once you are a millionaire, but, instead, once you change your mindset, becoming a millionaire will become possible.

In order to establish your millionaire destination point, you've got to know how your life would be different if money were no object. When I asked individuals or groups of people the simple question, "What would you do differently in your life if money were no object?" they generally laugh and dismiss the question as absurdly simple or nonsensical. But when I force them to really focus on the question, the answers do not come so easily.

One of the countless people I have met through *The Ultimate Gift* book and movie is the largest single lottery winner in America. This gentleman was instantly faced with the perplexing question of what he was going to do with all that money. Although it makes a good example for my point, I don't recommend playing the lottery, nor is the lottery mentality beneficial if you want to become or remain a millionaire.

Statistics show us that lottery winners are more likely to be bankrupt several years after receiving their winnings than they would have been had they never won the lottery. This is because they change their financial condition without changing their mindset.

Once you develop the millionaire mindset and begin following your millionaire map, your financial future will be secured even though you may currently have a negative net worth. On the other hand, if you are instantly given millions of dollars through the lottery or some other artificial means, it's only a matter of time until your mindset dictates your wealth, and you will be broke again.

All millionaire map destinations are custom made. We will study the various methods people use to become millionaires later in this book, but their destinations are as varied and personalized as the thousands of individuals who have become millionaires. Your reason for becoming a millionaire must be your own. You can't reach someone else's goal or live someone else's dream.

It is, however, important that your family members and the significant others in your life are on board with your millionaire map destination. These are the people on your team who are going to take this journey with you. They will be called on to make sacrifices and will be the people to encourage you and cheer you on to your destination.

As you're formulating your destination by asking yourself the powerful question, "What would I do if money were no object?" ask this of your family members and significant others so they can share in your goals and dreams.

As a young college student rapidly losing my sight, I was having regular mentoring sessions with my only millionaire friend at the time, Lee Braxton. He had what I thought was the annoying habit of giving me a thick book to read at the conclusion of each of our meetings. He didn't seem to want to take into consideration the fact that I was a college student with more than enough to read, and I was rapidly approaching total blindness so I was unable to see the books he gave me. Somehow, Crystal and I found the time to read each of those books, and they were the beginning of my lifelong love affair with books.

My friend and colleague Zig Ziglar often says, "Poor people have big TVs and small libraries while millionaires have

big libraries and small TVs." With all due love and respect
to my friend and mentor Zig Ziglar, I have found that millionaires have huge libraries and also have giant TVs if they
want them. Being a millionaire is not about having or not
having certain things. It's all about choices.

I heard a radio announcer discussing the fact that it was
payday, and he lamented, "My wallet is like an onion.
Every time I open it up and look inside, I cry." Countless
people heard that radio announcer's joke, and I'm certain
related to the sentiment, not because they want a leather
wallet full of paper with pictures of dead presidents. They
relate to the announcer's joke because of what the money
or lack of money means in tangible terms for themselves
and their families.

Mr. Braxton and the books he gave me began to convince
me that I needed some financial goals. He assured me that
paying my bills and eating on a regular basis was not a millionaire destination.

Since I was a college student living in a dormitory, my first
thought about millionaires living in mansions didn't really
relate to me as a short-term realistic goal; but my second
thought of the millionaire lifestyle involved wonderful and
expensive automobiles. That goal did relate to me as Crystal and I, at that time, were getting around in a 10-year-old
Pontiac lovingly known as The Green Dog.

I mean no offense to anyone who has ever driven a green
car or a 10-year-old Pontiac. I don't even want to offend
any dogs. While we were thankful to have the car at all,
when I thought of my millionaire goals and visualized my
financial destiny, The Green Dog was not in the picture.

Our car wasn't exactly green. It was a two-tone model that you may be familiar with which included green and rust. The trunk leaked, and our best efforts to stop or reduce the flow all failed, so I permanently solved the issue by drilling holes in the bottom of the trunk so at least the gallons of water that flowed into the trunk would drain out the bottom.

While in college, I was training as an Olympic weightlifter, and the university had a track team. The coach sought me out as they were desperately in need of a shot-putter and discus thrower. The coach didn't know if I had any experience but he thought being an Olympic weightlifter was a good place to start.

My first throw of the shot put convinced the coach that I had a future, and I was instantly on the track team. Crystal drove me to practice each day with the 16-pound shot put rolling around in the trunk of The Green Dog. As she rounded corners, it would roll across and hit the inside of the trunk, resulting in us having the only rusted-out, leaking, 10-year-old Green Dog that dented out.

We began looking for the kind of car we would want to drive when we reached our millionaire destination. We were thrown off of several car lots by sales people who instantly surmised that two college students driving the rusted Green Dog with the convex dents were not going to buy a luxury automobile or expensive sports car.

We were undaunted. In fact, several of their rude comments really motivated us. It certainly made it a pleasant experience when, a few short years later, Crystal and I drove up in The Green Dog and paid cash for the Mercedes we had been dreaming about. We had to donate The Green Dog to a charitable organization in the area because the dealer wouldn't even take it on a trade-in.

We often think of The Green Dog and wish we still had it. Not to drive around in, but to be reminded of the beginning of our millionaire journey.

We enjoyed that Mercedes so much, every car we have owned since that time has been a Mercedes. You may or may not like Mercedes, but as I mentioned earlier, becoming a millionaire is not about any specific thing. It's about choices.

While we were looking at one of our subsequent Mercedes, the car dealer showed us a Rolls-Royce. It's amazing how your reception improves when you drive up in a Mercedes instead of a Green Dog. We looked at the Rolls-Royce and agreed it was a wonderful car, but it cost three times as much and while we could have easily afforded it, we liked the Mercedes better.

Remember, it's your goal and your destination. It doesn't matter what anyone else thinks.

Recently, I was enjoying a TV profile on Warren Buffett. The young lady interviewing Buffett for the feature traveled from New York to Omaha to spend a day with the famous investor and financial icon. She was pleasantly surprised when Warren Buffett, himself, picked her up at the airport, but she was a bit puzzled and stated, "I'm shocked you drive a three-year-old Lincoln."

Buffett just shrugged, and she asked, "Can you tell us why you drive this car?"

Buffett shared some valuable wisdom with her as well as you and me when he said, "I'm not willing to buy anything, drive anything, or do anything simply to impress you."

During a speaking engagement in Omaha, I had some spare time one afternoon and made the pilgrimage over to the Buffet Building. I have stayed in Trump Tower, had meetings in the Forbes Building, and visited a myriad of very impressive buildings, but the Buffett Building is not among them. Mr. Buffett has obviously found his millionaire motivators other than within goals of cars and buildings. Recent news items would indicate Mr. Buffett's millionaire destination includes being one of the largest philanthropists in recorded history. The fastest way to never reach your millionaire destination is to try to convince everyone that you're already a millionaire.

I live in Oklahoma in the middle of cattle ranch country. A popular trend in western wear and cowboy wardrobe began when John Travolta made the movie *Urban Cowboy*. For a few hundred dollars, you can dress like people who don't know any better think millionaire ranchers dress. The real wealthy ranchers have a saying about those Travolta lookalikes. They laugh and scornfully announce, "He's all hat and no cattle."

When it comes to achieving your millionaire status, or any other significant goal in your life, the first and only person you need to impress is yourself.

The first element of your own millionaire destination that you visualize may not be something you want. It may be, like I experienced, something you don't want. More than the wonderful home, great cars, and amazing trips we continue to enjoy, my most prized millionaire possession is knowing that I will never again have that feeling that came over me when Crystal had to put a single loaf of bread back on the shelf.

Your ongoing millionaire goals and the destination you visualize, like mine, will include many things you want to do for other people and organizations that are important to you.

Shortly after Crystal and I got out of college, we began our millionaire quest. One of our first milestones of financial success enabled us to start a scholarship fund with some other university alumni. Over the last 25 years, we have been pleased that that little seed which came out of our millionaire destination goal has helped to send over 500 young people to college.

I remember walking across that college campus years ago as a student talking with Mr. Braxton about my millionaire destination. At that time, Crystal and I weren't sure we could pay for our own education, much less provide tuition, room, and board for hundreds of other students.

Mr. Braxton enjoyed walking with me across campus and stopping to sit on a bench in front of one of the dormitories. The sign over the door read Braxton Hall. He always told me that if all your goals in your millionaire destination are only about you, it's never enough.

He explained, "The best thing you can do for poor people is not be one of them. Not all rich people help poor people, but at least they have the choice, whereas no poor people can help poor people."

I think of Mr. Braxton often, and even though he passed away many years ago, as I continue to experience the millionaire journey he helped me start, I feel as if he is still with me. I wish we could meet today on that same bench outside Braxton Hall so I could tell him everything he made possible. If I could have that conversation with him today, I would ask him to walk a little farther across campus with me and show him the new Stovall Administrative Center on that same campus where he and I walked and talked so many years ago when I couldn't even pay attention, much less pay for a major building project.

Becoming a millionaire is not just about all the things you want to have, but it's about the things you want to do and give. I enjoy giving away $100 bills. I often pay school kids $100 for one-page reports on books I think they ought to read. It won't surprise you to learn most of these kids get their first $100 from me for reading *Think and Grow Rich*. I call them Franklin Awards because the $100 bill pictures Ben Franklin on it.

Unlike most everyone else memorialized on our currency, Ben Franklin wasn't a politician. He was an inventor, a publisher, an entrepreneur, and a self-made millionaire. I have had the privilege of giving many waiters and waitresses my Franklin Awards, and I have surprised a number of hotel maids with $100 tips by way of thanking them for their outstanding service or great attitude.

My motivation is not to prove to anyone I'm a millionaire but, instead, I want to prove to them that their own value and worth is far greater than they might have thought.

Enjoy the process of visualizing your millionaire destination. It will expand your mind in ways you never could have imagined, and if you haven't figured it out yet, you can't expand your wallet until you expand your mind.

CHAPTER SIX

Millionaire Myths

As you're traveling the route set out on your millionaire map, avoid the mirages.

HOPEFULLY, YOU HAVE BEEN BUSY beginning to visualize all of the things that will make up your millionaire destination. You've probably been thinking about magnificent homes, wonderful cars, fabulous clothes, exciting trips, and all of the things you want to do for friends, family, and causes that are important to you.

Before you move forward, there is one final step you need to undertake in order to fully establish your millionaire destination. You've got to begin to calculate a cost for each element which, combined, will give you your destination number. Your wishes and dreams will begin to go from fantasy to realistic goals on your millionaire map when you start putting a price on everything.

When Crystal and I started looking at Mercedes while we were still driving The Green Dog, it went from a fairy tale to a realistic destination on our own millionaire map once we began looking at the sticker prices of the various cars.

Your destination number will include the costs of all the things you want to have, do, and give away as well as the amount of money it will take to generate a return large enough for you to make a living. In this way, your money will start working for you instead of you working for your money. One nice benefit I discovered when my money started working for me was the fact that I only could work 60 or 70 hours a week but my money works around the clock every day.

Your destination number will change throughout your life, but you've always got to have that number in your mind. You've gone through the process of determining where you are financially as well as the establishing of where you want to be, but your destination number will quantify how far the two points are from one another on your millionaire map.

This process will make you start feeling like a millionaire even though you may still have a negative net worth. As those images of your goals and dreams come into focus and materialize as a concrete destination, it is vital that you come to understand who and what millionaires are and, just as importantly, who and what they are not.

We now reach the point at which you are going to have to begin making the biggest change in your life that will be required for you to become a millionaire. This revolutionary change will not initially come in how you earn, save, manage, or invest your money. The big change you are going to have to master in order to become a millionaire will reside in your mind.

For many years in my books, movies, syndicated columns, and speeches, I have warned millions of people about the dangers of what I call "The Big Lie." The Big Lie would tell us that there are two kinds of people in the world. There are healthy, wealthy, happy, and successful people that get everything they want out of life, and then there are people just like you and me who work hard and never really get anywhere.

The Big Lie would have you seeing yourself as a hamster in a cage, running faster and faster on the little wheel, but never really getting anywhere in your personal or professional life. If you believe this Big Lie, it becomes true, but if you reject it, you can live the life of your dreams, and you will join me on the quest to warn others about The Big Lie.

Adolf Hitler, who I have never before found an appropriate place in one of my books to quote, said, "If you tell a lie long enough and loud enough, it becomes reality."

A lot of skeptics would tell you that the facts are all that matter. I believe that when your dream is big enough, the facts simply don't count, and you and I always have a choice regarding how we are going to perceive and act upon the so-called facts.

The majority of people in our society today apply The Big Lie to the concept of reaching financial independence, becoming a millionaire, and living out their dreams. These people believe that millionaires inherited their money, won the lottery, got lucky, or were the beneficiary of some other external force that brought them millions of dollars. Eliminating this one belief from your life is the biggest single factor in you reaching your millionaire destination.

I remember reading a story about immigrants from Europe who came to America in the mid-19th century. Europe had been undergoing a famine and horrific economic times. People believed then, as they do today, that America represents the land of opportunity where dreams come true.

I read the diary accounts of one particular family who was barely scratching out a subsistence living in London. They held the belief that if they could get to America, their future would be brighter.

The father, mother, and three children began saving every bit of money they could possibly find in order to purchase passage on a sailing ship to America. They just didn't sit around and think about going to America or dream about it, they took action and began saving their money.

The father began contacting everybody he could to find out how much the trip might cost and if there were any special arrangements he might find to make the voyage affordable for his family.

After several years of scrimping and saving, the father met a captain of a ship that would be sailing to America in just a few days. The captain explained that they had been expecting some cargo to arrive that was scheduled to be transported to New York below decks, but if the cargo did not make it to the dock before the ship sailed, this father, his wife, and their three children could make the trip to America below decks in the cargo hold.

The family had not only been planning and dreaming, they had been earning and saving to reach their destination, and when it was time to act upon their dreams and move toward their destination, they were ready to pull the trigger. A lot of people wish, plan, dream, and even make preparations, but when the door to their destination swings open, they do not step through the door, pull the trigger, and act on their dreams. This family in London was resolute, however, and when the cargo did not arrive as the ship was preparing to sail, the father, mother, three children, and all of their worldly possessions were at the bottom of the gangway, ready to board the ship and take on the journey toward their dreams they believed awaited them in America.

Purchasing the passage for the voyage, even in the cargo hold, had taken virtually all of their money. The family loaded all of their worldly possessions into the cargo hold and made themselves comfortable as possible for the long and arduous voyage.

During their brief time rushing across the decks to load their luggage and possessions, they couldn't help but notice all of the prosperous-looking people dressed in finery enjoying the bon voyage party on the upper decks. The ship that the family was sailing on was a luxury liner that offered the most well-appointed and upscale suites and cabins anywhere.

The family felt the excitement building as the ship sailed out of London, and they headed into the North Atlantic for the voyage toward their destiny.

The ship experienced stiff headwinds, and the trip to America was taking several days longer than had been planned. The meager portions of food and water that the family had been able to afford and pack away among their belongings were rapidly consumed. The father and mother became

THE Millionaire Map

more distressed as their food and water dwindled. They shared increasing amounts with their children from their own rations until the last morsels of food and the last drops of water were gone.

As their children slept, the father and mother could see through the cracks between the boards of the deck above them that there was a sumptuous banquet going on right over their heads. They lamented their plight as they watched their children slowly starving with the most sumptuous display of delicacies literally within a few steps from where they lay starving.

Finally, in utter desperation, the father slipped out of the cargo hold and approached one of the ship's officers. He pleaded, "I know my family and I could only afford passage to America in the cargo hold, and we are not living in one of your luxury suites or cabins, but would it be possible for me to take some of the scraps of food that your kitchen boys are throwing overboard to the seagulls, for me to feed my starving children?"

The ship's officer was incredulous as he explained, "Sir, your quarters on this ship were, indeed, limited to the cargo hold, but the food served on deck at each meal is prepared by the greatest chefs in the world and is made up of the finest cuisine anywhere. It is now, and always has been, available to all of our passengers, including you and your family."

This family traveling to America to pursue their dreams nearly starved to death and could have easily died during the voyage. This near tragedy was not a matter of there not being any food, the food not being available to the family, or them not being able to enjoy it any time. Their looming starvation was caused by a single belief that they held. This family and all of their dreams might have died because they believed that the people on deck were somehow different and entitled to all of the good things that were available while their family was somehow different and had to suffer the consequences.

If you believe that millionaires are different from you, your life will be filled with financial starvation while everyone around you enjoys an economic banquet. Let's set aside your previous beliefs, assumptions, and the prevailing millionaire myths and just look at the facts.

Money is among the most misunderstood commodities in our society; therefore, millionaires are among the most misunderstood people. If you believe the popular myths, you will distort your millionaire map and make it impossible to follow your route to your destination.

The myth would tell us that millionaires inherited their money, won the lottery, have some unique talent or intelligence, stumbled into a miraculous investment, or received millions from some other mysterious, incomprehensible source unavailable to you. In reality, 90 percent of millionaires today are first generation. To paraphrase the old TV ad, "They made their money the old-fashioned way. They earned it."

Most of today's millionaires did not even enjoy a particularly high income. Seventy percent of millionaires today own their own small business or are self-employed. The majority of millionaires are not made up of Fortune 500 CEOs working from their ivory-tower offices. The majority of millionaires have lived in the same house for over 20 years, do not drive the current model automobile, and could go a decade or more without working.

Many millionaires could live their current lifestyle or greater and never work again. These millionaires are truly financially independent. They understand that money creates choices, and they are no longer going to be in a position where they are forced to trade their time, effort, and energy for someone else's money.

They look upon their net worth like a cow that produces milk that can nourish and feed them from now on. They can spend, enjoy, give away, or waste the milk, but they never touch or let anyone harm the cow.

Millionaires, like other groups of people, don't look or act as they are depicted in movies and television. Most millionaires do not own a yacht or a private jet, although many of them could if they wanted to.

While we're dispelling the myths of who millionaires are and how they got their money, we need to examine the myths regarding how millionaires spend their money. The majority of palatial homes, luxury automobiles, expensive clothes, and jewelry, are not purchased by the millionaires. They are purchased by people who want to look like they are millionaires.

As we explored earlier, money is about choices, and if you choose to spend all of your money looking as if you're wealthy instead of truly becoming wealthy, this is your choice, and I would not try to dissuade you. This is a book about becoming rich, not becoming happy. If you're not happy now, you never will be unless you change your attitude, not your net worth.

The ridiculous availability and access of easy credit has made it possible for people with virtually no net worth and relatively-modest income to appear to the uninitiated public to be wealthy. These are the people we talked about earlier who prefer to be all hat and no cattle.

While this may temporarily stroke something in your ego, when it comes time to enjoy a family meal, millionaires would rather eat a beefsteak than a cowboy hat.

The proverbial headlong quest to keep up with the Joneses has kept many people from becoming truly wealthy.

Several years ago, Crystal and I moved into what was then our dream home. We had been looking at houses in the neighborhood for quite some time.

I grew up near that area, geographically, but light years away economically. When I was in grade school, the land where our current neighborhood is located was a picturesque horse ranch with a scenic pond at the bottom of a gently-sloping hill. Our home where we currently live sits on that hill and has a wonderful view of the pond and much of the city.

It is in the upper one percent of houses in our area with respect to property value. It's not the most expensive home in town as we have looked at that home and could have afforded it but prefer where we now live.

When we moved into our dream home in our current neighborhood, we started meeting many new friends and neighbors. Some of our neighbors have a lot of cattle, and others have a really big, fancy hat. I will never forget going to meet a family who lived in one of the most prominent neighborhoods in our city. From the outside, you would have presumed that this was the home of a multimillionaire or even decamillionaire family; however, a brief look inside revealed the house was furnished with folding lawn chairs and garage sale furniture.

For many years, my home had lawn chairs and garage sale furniture, but I wasn't living in a million-dollar mansion. As we have said, money is about choices, and if this family wants to create the façade of wealth, that is their business; but we were saddened and truly grieved for them when their house was foreclosed upon, and they were forced into bankruptcy.

I don't recommend anyone live the "All hat, no cattle" life, but if you're going to, at least keep up the payments on your hat. Nothing will keep you poor more than trying to appear as if you are a millionaire. Ironically, the true millionaires appear surprisingly normal from the outside looking in.

Most families in America are currently 30 to 60 days from bankruptcy. This is to say that if you suddenly shut off their income, they are going to go into default mode in one or two months. This condition does not only affect lower- and middle-income families but many of the families with the highest incomes in our society seem to want to spend every dime they have to create the wealth façade.

As we will discuss in a later chapter, in order to become a millionaire and live the true millionaire lifestyle, you're going to have to spend less than you earn. The amount of your wealth will be determined, to a greater extent, by what you end up spending more than how much you eventually earn.

In my study of millionaires, I have run across people of all income, social, and educational backgrounds. Becoming a millionaire is not a matter of where you came from yesterday or who you are today. It is a product of what you do tomorrow that counts.

The average millionaire lives on 10 percent or less of their net worth. This is to say that the average family with a net worth of $2 million spends less than $200,000 each year. Please keep in mind that when you have a net worth of $2 million and no debt of any kind, therefore no payments, $200,000 will go a long way. In fact, you might find it challenging to spend it all.

We have all read the inspiring stories, and I've studied extensively the statistics of first-generation immigrants who come to America virtually penniless and become millionaires within one generation. These are the people who do not, in many cases, speak our language or fully understand our culture. They have not had the educational, social, or economic benefits that many of us have enjoyed. These new arrivals become millionaires because they believe in their dreams and have not bought into the millionaire myths that plague many of us born in this country.

Ironically, the children and grandchildren of these millionaire immigrants who have the educational and cultural advantages that we would find more typical here in our country, do not become wealthy as rapidly or predictably as their parents and grandparents. These offspring of millionaire immigrants perform economically much like native-born Americans. They still believe that millionaire dreams can come true because they've seen it in their own family. They fail to become millionaires themselves because they take on the spending habits of our culture. They become much more interested in looking rich than truly accumulating wealth.

It's often hard to tell the real millionaires at first glance, particularly when economic times are good; however, once there's a recession or the stock market has a temporary pullback or layoffs occur, those who are all hat and no cattle become apparent.

Warren Buffett may have said it best when he stated, "You can't tell who's swimming naked until the tide goes out."

Approximately 3 percent of the people in our society become millionaires. This may be discouraging to some who might calculate their odds of becoming a millionaire to be approximately one in 30; their calculations would be inaccurate, however, since I believe after studying many millionaires and becoming one myself, if you are willing to banish the millionaire myths from your life, not try to look like a millionaire while you're becoming one, determine where you are on your millionaire map as well as where you want to be, and start out on a systematic, predictable journey, your odds of becoming a millionaire are virtually certain.

Becoming a millionaire is not a three-strikes-and-you're-out proposition. As a blind person myself and an avid follower of Major League Baseball via satellite radio, I am convinced that I could get a hit off of the best Major League pitcher if you will allow me to alter only one of the rules of the game. If you will just give me an unlimited amount of strikes, and I can therefore swing as many times as I want, I will succeed as long as I keep swinging and don't quit. As the baseball legend Yogi Berra once stated, "It ain't over 'til it's over."

A great African explorer said, "The hunter can make many mistakes but the hunted can only make one." Your millionaire quest is a matter of focus and persistence.

Millionaires are mostly entrepreneurs and small-business owners. They control their destiny. They actually fail in business at a greater rate than the national average, but they keep plodding ahead on the simple journey indicated by the course on their millionaire map.

Unless you control your own map and create your own vehicle, the odds of getting where you want to go are pretty remote. If you're riding in someone else's vehicle, you are predictably going to end up at their destination and not yours.

If you will remember who millionaires really are and how they got there, you will find it quite easy to join them.

CHAPTER SEVEN

Your Millionaire Route

While you will have only one current position and one destination on your millionaire map, there can be an infinite number of routes.

I remember as if it were yesterday my earliest meetings with Lee Braxton as he gave me the foundations of my millionaire journey. I kept asking the simple question, "How do I get rich?"

Mr. Braxton simply implored me to be patient, and he continued to go through the concepts we have been exploring in this book including: Who are millionaires? Where do they come from? Who you should take advice from as well as who you should avoid, misconceptions about millionaires, and all of the other things you and I have explored in the first six chapters. You have probably been asking yourself the same question I kept asking myself when Mr. Braxton was giving me the basics. "When is this guy going to tell me how to become a millionaire?"

The answer is: Right now.

Please understand that everyone who becomes a millionaire and maintains the millionaire lifestyle masters the concepts of offense and defense. In this chapter, we're going to discuss offense. This is to say, how most millionaires make their money. Remember, virtually all Americans have enough income throughout their lives to be a millionaire if they learn how to save and invest. Conversely, no matter how much money you earn, you can blow it if you don't master the defensive concepts we will discuss in a later chapter; but for now, let's look at how millionaires get their money.

As we have discussed, only 10 percent of millionaires inherit their money. If you are among those lucky souls who won that gene-pool lottery, congratulations for becoming a millionaire, and please read the coming chapters carefully that deal with the defensive concepts of saving and investing.

Once you are a millionaire, your focus must shift from getting rich to staying rich. You don't want to fumble on the proverbial goal line.

Now, for everyone else, it's time to learn how to become millionaires in the same way that 90 percent of all millionaires achieved their financial goals. Nine out of 10 millionaires earn their money.

When I hear people talk about "making" money, I cringe because the only people who make money work in a mint. The rest of us will earn our money. This is an important distinction as the only long-term, consistent way to earn money is to create value in the lives of others.

Among the 90 percent of self-made, first-generation millionaires, the majority own their own business, or are entrepreneurs. Fully 70 percent of people who currently enjoy a millionaire lifestyle earned their money by becoming entrepreneurs or owning their own business.

You may be asking, "Ok, if 10 percent inherited their money, and 70 percent are business owners and entrepreneurs, what about the remaining 20 percent?" This 20 percent of millionaires are made up predominantly of corporate executives, middle managers, or specialized employees who achieve a moderate to high income and become very successful savers and investors.

At first glance, becoming someone else's employee may appear to be the more safe and prudent course of action, and for many people it is, indeed, the best way to go; however, you must explore the risk. While it is true that many self-employed people fail, they have the privilege of dusting themselves off and starting over, thereby swinging at the ball until they hit a home run.

Employees have the security of a regular paycheck, often with attractive benefits; however, they do not control their own destiny, and many people standing in the unemployment line thought they were safe and secure.

I am a firm believer that the only way to earn money is to create value for others, and the only true security is in your ability to perform. Non-performing, self-employed people who do not create value for others will find themselves out of business very quickly, but employees who are not creating value for their employers are simply treading water before they inevitably go over the falls.

Everyone who earns money is inevitably dependent upon an entrepreneurial venture to one degree or another. If you are self-employed, this is obvious. If you work for a corporation or the government, it may not be so apparent, but it is, nevertheless, true.

All corporations, no matter how large, represent someone's entrepreneurial venture. The enterprise, as a whole, is subject to the same rules and, therefore, the corporation only survives to the extent that it creates value in the lives of real people.

Finally, there are people who work for the government who mistakenly assume they have a safe and secure income regardless of their performance. While this may temporarily appear to be the case, in the final analysis, they will only survive if they create value for others.

Government workers are paid from taxes. Taxes come directly or indirectly from entrepreneurs. There is no money until value is created, and this value is inevitably created by an entrepreneur who provides services or products for which people are willing to exchange hard-earned money.

For over a decade, I have worked with groups in Washington, DC, who analyze and spend our tax dollars. I always laugh, either silently or sometimes out loud, when I hear bureaucrats in the government refer to "government money." I understand what they are trying to say, but it's important to realize there is no such thing as "government money."

At this point, I hope you are coming to the inescapable realization that if you are going to be a millionaire you are going to have to earn money through creating value for other people. This is an exciting concept when you think about it. A lot of people who work in the nonprofit area, which is also funded directly or indirectly by entrepreneurs, take great satisfaction in the fact that they make a difference in people's lives.

I support and do work for a number of worthwhile nonprofit organizations, and I am proud of the difference that they make in people's lives; however, when I go to work every day as an entrepreneur, I also make a true and lasting difference in people's lives. When you understand that the bigger the difference you can make in the lives of greater numbers of people, the more money you will earn; therefore, becoming a millionaire is a function of performing great service for other people.

If you work for someone else, you are a part of their entrepreneurial venture, and you will be providing a service for them directly and the people whom they serve indirectly. If this is your millionaire vehicle, as we've stated, you will need to be an aggressive saver and investor because the venture, itself, is designed to make the entrepreneur and the stockholders wealthy, not you.

When you are an employee, you are a commodity, and commodities are always judged based on price. If someone comes along, either domestically or internationally, who will do your job better or cheaper, it's only a matter of time until you find yourself out of work.

Becoming an entrepreneur or business owner means that the venture or enterprise exists to create wealth for you although that wealth may not be coming your way for weeks, months, or even years. Being an entrepreneur means that you do a lot of work you don't get paid for so that, someday, you can get paid for a lot of work you didn't do.

Employees harvest other people's crops. Entrepreneurs plant seeds. Employees will receive a smaller portion of the harvest on a regular basis. Entrepreneurs will receive the remaining profits from the entire harvest if and when it comes in.

Only 20 percent of people in America identify themselves as self-employed, business owners, or entrepreneurs, but of the 3 million people who have achieved and are living the millionaire lifestyle, fully 70 percent identify themselves as either self-employed, entrepreneurs, or business owners.

For the vast majority of people reading this book, this will be your vehicle to your millionaire destination.

I remember as a small child going to a Civil War battlefield with my grandparents. On one edge of a large open area, there was an authentic Civil War cannon and, beside the cannon, was a pile of cannonballs. One of the activities that the tour guides offered to children touring the Civil War battleground with their families was an hourly cannonball race.

This involved each child being given a cannonball and racing to see who could get their cannonball from one end of the battlefield to the other and back again. These cannonballs were very heavy. A few of the larger kids could carry them a little ways, but then would be forced to stop and rest before they picked up their cannonball and carried it a bit further.

Some of the smaller kids simply rolled their cannonball along the ground. This proved to be a very effective technique in the cannonball race. After the race was over, the winner had been announced, and all of the cannonballs had been piled up again next to the cannon, a gentleman appeared wearing an authentic Civil War uniform. He showed all the kids and their families how to load the cannon and fire it. I'll never forget the thundering roar that exploded from that cannon as that heavy cannonball was shot the length of the entire battlefield. Those images stayed with me when I began learning how to become a millionaire through my entrepreneurial efforts.

When I got out of school, the vast majority of my classmates got jobs and began acquiring mortgages, car payments, and all of the other trappings of the modern-day lifestyle. This is normal and typical because 97 percent of people will not become millionaires. I, on the other hand, began floundering around trying to learn how to become an entrepreneur and launch my first venture.

As my classmates were rapidly rolling their cannonballs or carrying them across the battlefield, I was standing at the starting line trying to learn how to build and operate a cannon. If you had taken a snapshot a month, a year, or even several years after we all began our race on graduation day, you would have been convinced that my classmates were outpacing me, and I could never catch up.

But then, I became the proverbial "overnight success" on the day my cannon was built, loaded, and ready to fire. Just as my classmates who were competing with me in the economic race of life were disappearing into the distance, my cannon roared to life, and the first cannonball whizzed past them as if they weren't even moving.

The great thing about building a cannon or an entrepreneurial venture is the fact that you only have to build it once. As my stunned classmates were trying to figure out what the explosion was and how my cannonball had instantly soared past theirs, I calmly loaded and fired the next cannonball, and it has never stopped. An important element of becoming and remaining a successful entrepreneur is the concept of maintaining your cannon and always resupplying your cannonballs.

Every farmer knows that an ear of corn represents a few bites of food today or seeds that will create many rows of cornstalks at harvest time, each of which is taller than the farmer and holds multiple ears of corn. If you eat your seed corn, you will have food for a day. If you plant your seed corn, and continue to replant a portion of it into the future, you can own acre upon acre of corn that can feed you and the world around you. Farmers who eat their seed corn, feed themselves. Those who apply entrepreneurial principles feed the world and often become millionaires as they create value for other people.

So you may ask, "What do entrepreneurs do, and what am I going to do to become a millionaire?" Just stay tuned, and it will become clear to you.

You might be alarmed to know that I don't have the answers for your specific situation; however, you'll be pleased to know that I have the questions, and you will have the answers necessary to create the vehicle to get from where you are to where you want to go.

Once you create a cannon, it can be fired many times or moved to another field and fired there. The Civil War cannon I saw on that battlefield tour years ago was over 100 years old and still functioned perfectly.

In our society when you meet a new person, you generally exchange the answers to two questions: "What's your name?" and "What do you do?" Entrepreneurs often struggle with the answer to the latter question.

I am an entrepreneur. I have never really done anything else, but it's hard to define to the vast majority of people who work for someone else. While they may be able to state, "I'm the sales manager for XYZ Corporation," I cannot define my career quite so easily. Today, my entrepreneurial ventures focus in five areas: books, television, movies, syndicated columns, and speeches. I own a number of other ventures ranging from a golf course to a software company and several things in between, but my working life today revolves around those five things.

A lot of struggling entrepreneurs confuse diversification with distraction. I like to think of my current operation as a four-sided pyramid that comes to a point at the top. The point is the activity I am working on at any given moment, but in order to fit my model, my current activity must support and be supported by the other four elements.

For example, at this exact moment, I am dictating the words that you are reading in this book. This book represents the point of the pyramid; however, within these pages, I will discuss my movies, television work, syndicated columns, and speeches which will result in many more people becoming aware of my efforts, and some will want to do business with me.

When this book is released, I will be able to promote it and make potential readers aware of it as I publicize my movies, through my television work, as well as in my columns and speeches. Everything supports everything.

This becomes possible once you create a base through your first venture. As you launch your first entrepreneurial effort, you will, invariably, be confronted by challenges and barriers. Your immediate response will be to abandon your current venture and launch another because, especially for entrepreneurs, the grass is always greener somewhere else.

Launching a second or third venture before the first one is self-sustaining is a bit like having multiple infants in the diaper stage at the same time. While it is survivable, most new mothers would tell you it's probably less than desirable and can really stink; therefore, your entrepreneurial success will come from a base of operation that will be your first venture.

How do you select this venture? Where do you find it? And how do you begin?

First of all, you need to realize there are no good or bad ventures. Entrepreneurial enterprises are like shoes. It's more a matter of size, style, material, and personal preference.

In the next chapter, you will begin to understand the personalized elements in your life that you will draw upon to create your millionaire vehicle. You will receive some tools that will help you clarify your strengths and preferences.

Always remember: When you set out to be an entrepreneur or self-employed business owner, you enter into a minority of the population. Furthermore, when you set a goal of being a millionaire, you are striving to reach the financial level that puts you ahead of 97 percent of everyone in society. For this reason, aspiring millionaires are often misunderstood, criticized, and ridiculed.

As we discovered in an earlier chapter, the prevailing perception would tell us that millionaires inherited their money or were lucky. When you set a goal to become a millionaire and launch a venture to take you to your destination, a lot of people won't like this because it holds a mirror of reality up to them and their life. They are forced to examine the possibility that reaching their goals and becoming a millionaire might be within their reach, and they are forced to admit they are responsible for their current economic station in life.

Be careful who you share your dreams and goals with because your attitude is a vital asset in your journey to your millionaire destination. No matter how hard you try to be circumspect about your goals and dreams, some people will invariably learn about your quest and take it upon themselves to criticize you. They often justify their negative venom with a preface designed to make themselves appear as if they are acting in your best interest. They declare, "I'm only telling you this for your own good..." Or, "I just don't want to see you hurt yourself or be disappointed..." Or the oldie but goodie, "I knew a guy once who tried to get ahead doing that, and he failed...."

Realize any time you begin to elevate yourself above those around you in any of life's pursuits, you become a target. You will want to avoid as many of these attacks as you can, and embrace the others as fuel for your vehicle as it travels the millionaire route to your destination.

Shortly after losing my sight, a gentleman visited my home, identifying himself as a caseworker from the State Offices of Visual Services. I had never heard of this particular government agency, but as I was depressed, anxious, and approaching the end of my emotional rope, I decided to let him into my house and listen to him. He informed me, in no uncertain terms, that I needed to adjust my ambitions downward and modify my expectations toward mediocrity. He made arrangements for me to visit a sheltered workshop which is a place where blind or disabled people can work at a below-minimum-wage income.

It is not my purpose to criticize these organizations or the benefits they may create. My experience was enlightening and has probably turned out to be worth several million dollars of my current net worth.

When I reached the sheltered workshop, the manager told me my options consisted of two potential career paths. One was cutting out pizza boxes and the other was attaching erasers to pencils. Since the pencil gig paid 15 cents an hour more, I selected that one.

After showing me how to put the pencil and the eraser in the clamp and attach the sleeve, they let me try it. My pencil broke, and the eraser fell on the floor and bounced away. I was frustrated and embarrassed as I crawled around on the floor trying to blindly find the elusive eraser. I had another of those magical moments like the one in the grocery store when I couldn't afford a loaf of bread. I realized whatever I was going to do, it wasn't going to be this.

Please understand I'm not criticizing people who put erasers on pencils nor the people who offer them opportunities. I'm simply saying you mustn't let anyone give you life, career, or millionaire advice who isn't a millionaire, and avoid people whose supposedly-helpful statements begin with "You can't," "You won't," or "You'll never." You can file those kinds of statements in your mental millionaire moments file. They can clarify your goals and re-energize your efforts for years to come.

I remember deciding to write my first novel after writing six successful nonfiction titles. I sent the draft of my first novel to the publisher of my previous book. They sent me a form rejection letter, and the editor of my previous nonfiction book called with the advice, "Stick to what you know."

I might have quit trying if they had just sent the form letter, but the "Stick to what you know" comment from the editor of my last successful book brought me to the fork in the road. I decided either he or I was going to be proven wrong, and I was not giving up until everyone in the publishing industry had turned down this book.

If I had to pick one element that exemplifies more millionaires than any other, it would be dogged persistence.

After many similar rejection letters, I finally got a call from the president of Executive Books, Charlie "Tremendous" Jones. Charlie was a successful writer in his own right and then had launched a successful publishing enterprise. He actually had his middle name changed to Tremendous after the success of his book *Life is Tremendous*. No one's name ever fit them better than Charlie's.

He published *The Ultimate Gift* and promoted it everywhere he went until his death a decade later. Charlie became the ambassador for that book, the subsequent movie, and its message. At this writing, *The Ultimate Gift* book and movie along with the sequel titles have grossed in excess of $100 million. I was already a decamillionaire from my other business ventures and entrepreneurial efforts before that book and movie, but *The Ultimate Gift* opened up a whole new world for me and the people I serve.

Several years later, I had the wonderful experience that many millionaires enjoy as they succeed. My previous publisher flew into town to meet with me. He explained they hadn't done a book with me in a while and really wanted to work with me. He went on to explain how disappointed they were that I had not given them the chance to publish *The Ultimate Gift* since they had published my previous titles.

Thankfully, I had my millionaire file of motivating mementoes handy. I was actually able to show him a copy of his publishing company's rejection letter to me and provide him with a copy to take back with him, suitable for framing.

Success needs no explanation, and failure will bear no excuse. Don't argue with your detractors or debate with the doubters. Just succeed, and the reality of your millionaire destination will speak for itself.

CHAPTER EIGHT

The Vehicle for
your Journey

*A millionaire map becomes a practical
reality when you develop your vehicle.*

I remember my first organized millionaire search. I had
learned from Mr. Braxton, the books he had given me,
and the other millionaire mentors I was beginning to
meet. I thought I knew a little about who millionaires
were and were not, but I had to be reminded the hard way
one more time.

Among my earliest entrepreneurial ventures was running
my own investment office for a New York Stock Exchange
member firm. Like most eager young brokers, I had heard
the training about "Just call on average business people and
families, and help them invest their money." But I knew
better, so I was looking for the proverbial whales who
would invest the big bucks. I formulated my strategy to
find these millionaire whales and planned to target country clubs, high-end restaurants, resorts, luxury car dealers,
and the like.

I remember being frustrated one day after wasting the entire morning trying to find whales at the country club. I was shocked to find a printed notice on the bulletin board in the locker room listing the members who were at least two months behind in their club dues. Some of the names on the list were people I had targeted as potential large-investment clients.

I went to a luxury car dealer who had dealt in high-end cars for many years. He listened politely to my plans to find high-dollar whale investment prospects, chuckled wisely, and gave me some advice. "Son, if you want to find truly wealthy people on a car lot, you don't go to the high-end luxury or sports cars. Most of them are heavily financed. The people you are looking for are over on the used-car lot, paying cash."

Once again, I was reminded that millionaires aren't who we think they are, and just because someone looked like my movie image of a millionaire didn't mean they had much or anything to invest.

I went back to the basics of what I had learned from pro-files of millionaires in books as well as conversations with my millionaire mentors. I hit pay dirt when I started calling small businesses at 6:30 a.m. every day. I found that the owners of the dry cleaners, pest control company, painting contracting business, coffee shop, and most other entrepreneurs were hard at work early in the morning, but their secretaries and gatekeepers weren't on the job yet.

At 6:30 in the morning, I could talk to these entrepreneur business owners in person, and I was shocked to find that most of them were already millionaires and the rest were rapidly on their way to reaching millionaire status.

If you believe in what 97 percent of people think millionaires are, you'll never be a millionaire yourself. On the other hand, if you will accept the definition of millionaires from the 3 percent of people who have already reached their goals, you are well on your way to your own millionaire destination.

Let's say, after reading this far, you are more committed than ever to becoming a millionaire, and you now believe that becoming a self-employed entrepreneurial business owner is the best way for you to get there. How do you pick the winner and best opportunity among all the businesses out there? Remember, there are no bad or good businesses, and people are succeeding financially in virtually every entrepreneurial arena.

Don't assume that you have to pick the perfect business opportunity the first time, and it will be your only venture throughout your life. Many of the businesses you explore and even start as an entrepreneur will fail. This doesn't mean that your millionaire map is invalid, and you can never reach your destination. You may have to get out your spare tire from time to time and repair a flat, but it doesn't mean your destination is not a reality for you and your family.

Most entrepreneurs who become millionaires find a venture that works for them after exploring a number of opportunities. They then use their first successful business as a platform from which to launch many diversified but interdependent, supportive operations. This works in much the same way as my business is designed as I described it earlier using the pyramid analogy.

One of the concepts you will need to master as you dip your toe into entrepreneurial ventures and explore the myriad of possibilities is the concept I call accelerating your point of failure. It is not a negative statement to tell you that you will, inevitably, experience temporary failure. The key to reaching your financial goals, as most millionaires do through entrepreneurial efforts, is to identify failure as quickly as possible and move on.

If you've ever been to the horse races, you know it's hard to pick a winner. If your horse doesn't win immediately, there's always another race just a few minutes away. If your horse collapses on the track, you can't afford to just keep beating the dead horse. You've got to dust yourself off, move on, and pick a winner.

I believe in the old adage: Failure is not final. Failure is fertilizer. I have learned more from some of my false starts than many of my successes. We all pay for our education, and temporary failure is the tuition that most millionaires have paid.

You will have many ventures and pursue many opportunities throughout your life. People on the outside looking in might think you jump around a lot and are not committed. In reality, you are an entrepreneur, and entrepreneurs find and develop opportunities that create value in the lives of others. They know that the more value they create for the greatest number of people, the more they will move toward their millionaire goals.

I always think it's sad when I find someone at one of my speaking engagements or a book signing that tells me, "I used to have dreams of being a millionaire, but I started a business and it failed."

This would be like a baseball player who says, "I made it to the Major Leagues but quit after I struck out my first time at bat."

When I study entrepreneurial business owners who have created their financial millionaire base from their first successful business, I find that they all have some common traits. They are persistent, energetic, focused, and passionate. Passion may be the most important element of entrepreneurial success. If you understand that you succeed by working hard, smart, and efficiently, you will understand that pursuing your passion is critical.

If you don't love what you do, you will be competing against people who do love their business. They will outperform you every time because their business is like their baby.

You may like all children and want to help all kids in need, but you will certainly do more for your own sons and daughters than anyone else. For your own children, you will extend yourself beyond the greatest limit you ever thought possible and then go further still.

The landscape of potential business ventures for entrepreneurs is virtually limitless. If you will look at the headings at the top of each page in a business directory or yellow page phone book, you will find hundreds of things that people are doing to become wealthy that may have never occurred to you.

You just start exploring by answering the simple questions, "What have you always wanted to do?" or "If you could do anything you wanted for your life's work, what would it be?"

Don't pick a business venture just for the money. Select an opportunity that gives you the feeling of making a real difference in the lives of people. If you remember that you can succeed in virtually any enterprise, and millionaires own businesses and entrepreneurial ventures in virtually every field of endeavor, you can feel comfortable in selecting a direction that makes you happy and one where you can make a difference.

You might ask, "Don't I have to have talent in the field or business area I select?"

I would agree that someone in your organization has to have talents and abilities, but it doesn't have to be you. I have a very gifted and talented team that works with me every day. From time to time, due to vacations or illness, one of these team members has to cover the work of another. They perform this balancing act seamlessly; however, there is no role or task in my operation, other than my own, that I can even begin to perform.

People generally excel in the areas of their passion and competency. Start considering the things you like to do on your vacation, and some of those elements will appear in your dream avocation.

The late, great George Burns was fond of saying, "If you enjoy your job, you will never work another day in your life." This should be in the forefront of your thinking as you explore entrepreneurial ventures.

As a competitive Olympic weightlifter, I spent endless hours training on technique and repetitive motion that would keep me in what I call the "power groove." The power groove is a narrow range of motion in which a weightlifter or other athlete experiences their greatest strength and best performance. If a weightlifter, baseball pitcher, golfer, or any other athlete gets a fraction of an inch out of their power groove, their world-class talents and abilities will appear average or mediocre very quickly.

I have explained my own business briefly in earlier chapters. Even though we work in the five key areas of books, movies, television, syndicated columns, and speeches, I always try to remember that I am truly in the message business. The various avenues of my business are simply delivery systems for the message business where I work. When I remember this, I succeed fabulously, and when I get away from my defined purpose and power groove, my efforts produce mediocre and ordinary results.

For example, after a decade of being one of the most successful corporate and arena speakers in the world, I have reached a point where I can make more money in an hour than many average families make in a year. This high rate of return and profitability is only possible because, for that hour, I am functioning in my power groove.

If, instead of giving the speech, I helped people find their seats in the arena, unload boxes of my books, or work the sound and light console, not only will I not earn an amazing return for my efforts, I will be summarily fired because

I can't perform those functions as well as the trained professionals that are on the job in the arena every day.

Several years ago, I had the privilege of meeting Steve Forbes through the release of my book and subsequent movie titled *The Ultimate Gift*. Mr. Forbes has become not only a fan and promoter of my message but a true friend and mentor to me. During each of my trips to New York, I always set aside some time to spend with Mr. Forbes. We often sit in the library in the Forbes Building and discuss a myriad of topics, but our topic of conversation usually settles on money, wealth, and millionaires. There is probably no one in our society today who understands and promotes wealth and capitalism better than Steve Forbes.

After writing several novels and working on the films based on my books, Mr. Forbes confronted me during one of our meetings about writing another business book. He pointed out something I had not noticed about my own career. My first six books were nonfiction titles about success, happiness, and my own experiences in business. Then I wrote *The Ultimate Gift*, and with the success of that book and movie and subsequent films, my next seven or eight titles were novels.

Mr. Forbes told me that if I were ever going to write more business or success books, I should get some out soon or there would be a whole generation of readers who only knew me as a writer of fiction through my novels and movies. He and I began discussing the message in *The Ultimate Gift* book and movie as it might relate to a nonfiction business book. My conversation with Mr. Forbes made me start thinking about the key elements to financial success in business.

One of the critical components to any organization's success is teamwork. When I considered the concept of building a team, I began thinking about who had as much expertise in organizational teamwork as Mr. Forbes had in the world of finance. The one and only name that came to mind was legendary Coach John Wooden.

Coach Wooden's winning records and national championships stand alone at the top of any ranking or study of the best teams of all time. I met Coach Wooden when he contacted me after reading one of my books. He was 96 years old at the time, and for the next three years until we lost him just short of his 100th birthday, Coach Wooden and I had a number of discussions about success, building a winning team, and making each day your masterpiece.

I took the inspiration and information from my mentors, Steve Forbes and Coach Wooden, and put it in a book called *Ultimate Productivity*. Steve Forbes wrote the foreword, and Coach Wooden's wisdom and experience abound throughout the book.

Ultimate Productivity deals with succeeding in business through motivation, communication, and implementation. Along with my colleague, Rebeka Graham, who is one of the best corporate and business trainers in the world working with Fortune 500 companies and business leaders throughout the U.S., Europe, and Asia, I developed a Productivity Profile that allows people to get an assessment of their entrepreneurial and business strengths, competencies, preferences, and passions.

Thousands of successful entrepreneurs and aspiring millionaires have taken the Productivity Profile and received their assessments. I would like to give you this gift now as my own contribution toward your millionaire map. Just log on to www.UltimateProductivity.com. Follow the prompts to take the Productivity Profile and enter your access code, 586404. The results should help you narrow down your entrepreneurial search toward your first millionaire venture.

Remember, whether your first venture succeeds or fails, you will always move on and acquire more business ventures and entrepreneurial opportunities. Your first venture may only serve to get your feet wet, or it may be the lifelong millionaire base you will use to build your own millionaire lifestyle.

My mentor, Mr. Braxton, left school in the third grade and began working with his brother in a bicycle repair shop in the small town where they lived in order to support their family. Mr. Braxton saved the nickels and dimes he earned each day in order to grow his own nest egg. He explained to me years later that a nest egg is the admission price to explore and acquire entrepreneurial business ventures. If you don't build your nest egg, it won't matter how great a deal you might find because you won't have the price of admission to get started. In order to pull the trigger, you've got to be able to afford a gun.

Mr. Braxton and his brother were moderately successful in their bicycle business. It was during the depths of the Great Depression, and they, like most people, were pleased to have any income along with food to eat.

I have always believed that success comes when opportunity and preparedness meet. Mr. Braxton was a young, teenaged entrepreneur in his bicycle repair business when his first home run venture came along.

The term "train wreck," literally and figuratively, denotes a disaster for most people in our society. A train wreck for Mr. Braxton was his first millionaire milestone, and he was ready, willing, and able to pull the trigger.

One day as Mr. Braxton and his brother were working in their bicycle shop, they heard an unbelievable explosion at the other end of their small town. They rushed down the street to find out what in the world might have happened.

They saw dust and smoke rising into the air near the railroad tracks, and as they arrived on the scene, they discovered there had been a train wreck. Thankfully, no one was badly hurt when the two freight trains met, but several freight cars had derailed and were lying on their sides near the edge of the track.

In order to make sure no one was injured, Mr. Braxton and his brother climbed through each of the freight cars on the train, including those lying on their sides next to the tracks.

Eventually, the police, firefighters, and railroad officials arrived on the scene, and finally, a gentleman in an expensive business suit approached Mr. Braxton and his brother and asked if they had seen the train wreck. They explained that they had not seen the wreck, itself, but had arrived shortly after and had gone through each of the cars looking for any people who might be injured.

After the businessman confirmed that there had been no fatalities or serious injuries, he asked Mr. Braxton and his brother about the extent of the damage to the cargo in the freight cars. They described the wreckage and damage to the best of their ability, and finally Mr. Braxton asked the businessman why he was so interested in all the details.

The stranger explained he was an adjuster for the railroad's insurance company and needed to place a value on the wreck and dispose of the salvage.

Mr. Braxton asked a fateful question about how they would dispose of all of the salvaged goods, and the insurance adjuster announced, "Son, I would take a few pennies on the dollar for anyone that could clean up this mess and buy the damaged inventory."

Almost 60 years later, Mr. Braxton described that moment to me. He explained, "Jim, if the church bells rang and the choir sang at that instant, it would not have been any more clear to me that this was my moment, and the years of hard work and savings had brought me to this time and place."

Mr. Braxton and his brother borrowed a tractor, pulled the damaged freight cars away from the railroad track, and invested their accumulated life savings from their business in the contents of those freight cars. Fortuitously, they purchased huge quantities of small appliances, including toasters, irons, mixers, and similar products.

Although Mr. Braxton's formal education had ended years before in the third grade, he read prodigiously and was an avid reader the rest of his life. He believed World War II was looming on the horizon and knew that America would have to devote all of its manufacturing capacity toward equipping the soldiers going to war. Mr. Braxton and his brother cleaned, repaired, and stored the thousands of small appliances they had just purchased, and they systematically became multimillionaires, meeting the needs of people for small appliances throughout the war years.

Mr. Braxton knew what you and I must understand, that sometimes our first venture, in his case the bicycle shop, is nothing more than the launch pad for the next venture and the one after that.

You don't always hit the home run your first time at the plate. Any good baseball manager will tell you most games are won by batters who just get the bat on the ball and get to first base. If you can just get a hit and worry about moving to the next base, sooner or later the home runs will come. Batters who try to hit a home run the first time, every time, generally strike out and are quickly out of the game entirely.

Trying to get rich quick on every venture is the best way I know to get poor and stay that way. Don't worry about your immediate return. Worry about creating value in the lives of others. If you focus beyond yourself and build your nest egg, sooner or later, your home run or train wreck will come.

It's vital that you enjoy the journey and pursue your passion. The player who enjoys the game and is passionate about hitting singles and moving to the next base is most likely to be in the game and waiting on second or third base when the home run comes and drives them in to score.

You must enjoy the balance between today and tomorrow.

I love to read and complete a book virtually every day. Among the many topics I enjoy exploring within the pages of books is mountain climbing, as I mentioned earlier. I have never climbed a serious mountain and probably never will. Mountaineering is probably not an appropriate pursuit for a blind, retired weightlifter; however, I enjoy the stories of dedicated people who work for years to mount expeditions and then climb the world's tallest peaks.

I believe it is instructive to you and me to realize that these people spend their life savings and years of effort to spend a few minutes on the top of the world. If they don't enjoy the journey, in addition to the peak experience, they are going to have a miserable life.

If you and I will simply focus on pursuing our passion and creating value in the lives of others, our millionaire destiny is virtually assured. On the other hand, if we buy into the "get rich quick" fad-of-the-month or the "overnight millionaire myths," we are destined to live a life of quiet desperation watching the successful people enjoy their millionaire lifestyles.

You need to start thinking of your entrepreneurial search as your current career. Exploring business opportunities and looking for value is what millionaires do every day. Too many people want to grab the first deal and become an instant millionaire. It simply doesn't work like that.

The time, effort, and energy you invest in due diligence is well spent. People who spend time studying a roadmap, instead of just barreling down the highway where they think they might want to go, are going to arrive safely at their destination.

People spend more time planning their 3-day weekend than they spend contemplating that which they are going to do for the rest of their lives. If you don't get anything else out of this book, I want you to realize that this life we're living right now is not a practice game. It's the World Series, the Super Bowl, and the Olympics all rolled up into one. If you will create and follow your millionaire map, you are inevitably going to reach your destination. Just pursue your passion and enjoy the journey.

You will invariably arrive at your destination, and if you're doing the right things along the way, you will be ready, willing, and able when the fortuitous train wreck happens. If Mr. Braxton and his brother had been more worried about looking like millionaires rather than truly becoming and living their lives as millionaires, they would have not built their nest egg and been ready when the home run millionaire opportunity presented itself.

The best child psychology tool I have ever studied that is a predictor of future success and happiness is called The Marshmallow Test. You simply have a small child sit at a table in a room by themselves. When you enter, you present them with one marshmallow, and you tell them that they can eat that marshmallow right now, or you will be back in a few minutes and give them two marshmallows.

The kids who are willing to wait on their marshmallows are the future entrepreneurial millionaires. Those who can't wait five minutes and demand to eat their marshmallow right now will spend their whole lives struggling to look like they are succeeding instead of living their dream life and arriving at their millionaire destination.

CHAPTER NINE

Drive Defensively

As you follow the route on your millionaire map, avoid the pitfalls, detours, and dangers.

MANY YEARS AGO, I STOPPED calculating my wealth solely based on the amount of money I accumulate. Living the millionaire lifestyle should never mean only accumulating money. It's a matter of the things money will buy, do for others, as well as the doors money can open.

One of the treasures that came into my life as the result of the success of my books and movies was my friendship with John Wooden. Coach Wooden and I met as he was approaching his 100th birthday, and I was approaching my 50th. It's an interesting perspective to have all of the thoughts and anxieties that go with turning 50 when you have a friend and mentor you speak with regularly who is approaching 100.

Coach Wooden was the undisputed master of developing teams and helping them perform at the highest possible level. If you want to know more about John Wooden, simply do a Google search for the greatest coaches or teams of all time.

Thankfully, I recorded many of my interviews and conversations with Coach Wooden. As I review them today and reconsider his wisdom and experience, I am struck by the fact that very little of what he had to say dealt with sports or basketball, and when he did talk about basketball, there was a direct analogy and application to life.

One piece of Coach Wooden's wisdom that applies to your and my millionaire map and how we proceed along the route toward our destination is his statement, "Defense and free throws are what win championships, but players like to practice three-point shots and dunks."

Everyone who has even contemplated the thought of becoming a millionaire wants to live the proverbial lifestyle of the rich and famous today and begin accumulating stuff immediately. This is a sure way to never reach your financial goals and live your millionaire lifestyle.

Virtually everyone reading this book will earn enough money throughout their life to become a millionaire, so as we're considering hitting your financial home run through your own business and entrepreneurial ventures, it is important to just hit the ball and move to first base.

Some people become millionaires spectacularly. They are the "overnight sensations" that have invariably been working for years behind the scenes on their millionaire map; but they spring to prominence like a skyrocket. Then there are people who become millionaires the slow and steady way just as the tortoise defeats the hare in the famous story.

I encourage you to build and develop rockets that will speed you to your millionaire lifestyle through your entrepreneurial ventures; however, I want to be sure you also have the safety and certainty of a tortoise plan.

I am always amazed at how many people who can't seem to pay their basic bills and expenses manage to regularly purchase lottery tickets. Now, if you are among the millions of people who regularly buy a lottery ticket for entertainment purposes, I'm not going to argue with you, but I find nothing entertaining about throwing hard-earned money out the window.

You have probably heard that you are more likely to get struck by lightning six times or get hit by a meteor from outer space than to win the lottery. I would certainly rather win the lottery than get struck by lightning or get hit by a meteor, but I would like to propose an alternative.

Using recent government statistics of consistent purchasers of lottery tickets, I find it ironic that if these same people who spend several hundred dollars a week on the lottery would just open a retirement account and place the money in an average-performing mutual fund, they would retire as millionaires.

Several years ago, I wrote one of my weekly syndicated columns that appears in newspapers, magazines, and online publications around the world, about this lottery versus retirement fund alternative. I received more calls, letters, and email responses to this one column than virtually any of the hundreds of columns I have written throughout the years. While everyone who contacted me assured me they had already fully funded their own retirement account, current reports of the record-breaking lottery totals tell me that we've got a long way to go with respect to prudent financial planning in our society.

Starting early is the key to financial success. I want to see you achieving your millionaire lifestyle and living out your dreams sooner than later, but isn't it nice to know that, no matter what happens, you can retire as a millionaire if you just start early, and put your proverbial lottery-ticket money into a retirement account.

You will never miss the money each month, and it can be automatically moved into your retirement fund. This is much like putting your millionaire vehicle on cruise control, so while you're building your entrepreneurial ventures, you know that if you don't touch the cruise control, you will inevitably arrive at your millionaire destination.

Whenever I speak to audiences about budgeting their money, the minute the word "budget" comes out of my mouth, I can hear a collective groan throughout the convention center or arena. Please understand that you, I, and everybody in the world are living and will continue to live on a budget. Some of us choose to control our money and make it do the things we want it to do for us and those we care about.

Other people live on a budget which is limited only by how much money they have or can borrow on a regular basis. These people choose to let money control them instead of them taking control of their money.

I had a dear friend and colleague who was my partner in several ventures. I knew he was making a great income that was approaching a million dollars a year. I was shocked one day when he asked my advice regarding his inability to accumulate any wealth. A brief review of his financial situation revealed that his wife was spending several hundred thousand dollars a year on clothes, jewelry, and other items she deemed essential. While my friend nor I had any problem with buying clothes, jewelry, or anything else a person decides to do with their money, her spending was keeping them from reaching all of their financial goals.

My friend was tragically killed in an automobile accident shortly before his 40th birthday. I was the executor of his estate, and thankfully, he had exercised great foresight and prudence with life insurance policies that could take care of his family forever.

When I sat down with his widow to lay out her financial picture, I was very pleased and relieved to be able to inform her that she and her children would have no debt and could enjoy a lifetime income of $15,000 per month. At that time, a $15,000 per month income would put her within the top 4 percent of households in America with respect to income.

I was stunned then and to this day as I am dictating these words as I think of her statement, "The children and I cannot begin to learn how to live on only $15,000 a month." I eventually caught my breath and was able to disagree with her and correct her false impression as I stated emphatically, "Well, I can promise you that you will either learn how to live on $15,000 a month now, or you will learn how to live on a fraction of that amount after you waste all of this money your late husband provided."

Living on a budget is not about doing without. It's a matter of making choices. I'm not asking you to sacrifice forever.

I'm asking you to sacrifice for a season that will make your millionaire lifestyle possible.

You might be shocked to know that after meeting with literally thousands of millionaires and billionaires, I have yet to meet any of these people of wealth who didn't live on a budget.

Remember, I don't advocate a budget to deprive you of the things you want. The budget is to give you the nest egg you need to travel your millionaire route through entrepreneurial ventures, business opportunities, and lifetime investments. If Mr. Braxton had not lived on a budget and built his nest egg, the train wreck would have meant nothing in his millionaire quest.

No team can win without great offense and defense. Most Americans fail to reach their financial goals, not because they don't have enough money. They fail because they don't play great defense and control the money they have.

You may think you and your family are poor right now. I am hoping to convince you that your household is not poor. It is poorly managed.

Whatever budget or financial plan you emerge with on your millionaire map, it is critical that every member of your team be on board. As I mentioned earlier, my late friend and colleague was earning a million dollar income, but his wife was more than capable of spending it all.

If you don't control your money, a bit of wealth will only buy you a ticket for admission into a bigger game where people spend even more money. If you don't control your budget, no matter how much you obtain, you will never be wealthy. You will just be among the big league spenders. I can promise you, in the big leagues they know how to spend a lot of money.

There is nothing you cannot buy or own as a part of your millionaire journey, but if you eat your seed corn today, you will starve later. If you save and plant your seed corn, you will grow cornstalks in many fields that will buy you everything you and your family ever wanted for yourselves and other people around you.

You will either voluntarily control your money now, or it will force its control on you later.

When I was a teenager, there was a commercial for motor oil. A mechanic who was standing in front of a car with a blown engine implored us to change our oil regularly by saying, "You can pay me now or pay me later."

Today as you build your millionaire map, your dollars are saying, "You can save me now or be forced to save me later."

I do not suggest you limit your spending for the sake of doing without. Once you understand that every dollar today can be hundreds or thousands of dollars later, you will look at your spending differently. As we have discussed, compounding is the 8th Wonder of the World, but you've got to get it working on your side instead of continuing to have compounding working for the credit card company.

Every discussion of compounding makes me think of the "Rule of 72." This financial tool provides a quick and easy way for you to determine how long it will take to double your money. You simply divide 72 by the rate of return you are receiving or anticipate receiving on your investments, and the resulting number lets you know how many years it will take to double your money. For example, if your mutual fund is growing at a 12 percent rate, it will take you 6 years to double your money: 72 divided by 12 equals 6.

You will understand the magic of compounding when you see one become two, which becomes four, then turns into eight, and eventually becomes 16. When you're earning and saving your money, you are only adding to your wealth, but when you compound, you begin multiplying.

Before you start creating your nest egg for your entrepreneurial ventures and millionaire investment fund, you've got to create a "rainy day" or "emergency" fund. Small financial crises or minor money emergencies are inevitable here in the 21st century. There are so many electronic and mechanical components in our lives it's only a matter of time until some of them break down or become obsolete.

Much of the challenge involved in becoming a millionaire is a matter of creating a millionaire mindset. You've got to stay focused on your goals and your millionaire destination. It is difficult, if not impossible, to be exploring your millionaire entrepreneurial ventures and launching your own business while you get repeated distractions and interruptions from a broken fuel pump, malfunctioning refrigerator compressor, or the ever-present leaky roof.

Once you reach your millionaire lifestyle, these former emergencies and crisis events become nothing more than a minor annoyance. Crystal and I often laugh in the same situations that used to make us literally cry.

Before we began our millionaire journey, one of these breakdowns prompted questions of anguish such as "What are we going to do?" Today, the exact same situation elicits a question much more like, "Who are we going to call for that?"

This emergency or rainy-day fund can make you begin to feel like a millionaire because it keeps the poverty reminders away from your attitudes and efforts.

It's easy to begin building your nest egg for your millionaire financial future when you see the current dollars that you have as representing seeds instead of stuff. I'm not trying to deprive you from buying every little thing you want to have today. I'm trying to convince you to proceed in such a way that will enable you to have every big thing you want as you reach your millionaire destination.

Several years ago, I wrote a book entitled *The Ultimate Financial Plan* with my coauthor Tim Maurer, C.F.P. Tim is among the greatest financial planning and investing minds practicing today. In our book, Tim wrote about Timely Tips, and I wrote about Timeless Principles. Both are critical if you are going to reach your millionaire destination.

One of the chapters in our book, *The Ultimate Financial Plan*, dealt with a man who, literally, spent a million dollars at Starbucks. If you think like 97 percent of the population who are non-millionaires, this will seem absurd to you; but if, on the other hand, you see dollars as seeds, and seeds as opportunities like the 3 percent of people who are already millionaires, it makes total sense that someone could spend a million dollars at Starbucks.

In our book, Tim simply reviewed one gentleman's daily spending on exotic coffee at Starbucks and calculated what those same dollars could have earned in an average performing investment. Whether you ever darken the door of a Starbucks or not, I want you to go through your checkbook and credit card statements for the past three months, and examine your spending. If you are like most people and families, you are in for quite a shock.

Most people who do not live on a millionaire map budget and control their own money are surprised to find that not only do they have a hole in the bucket they are trying to fill, they actually have several holes, therefore making it impossible to fill their bucket no matter how much water they pour into it.

One of the biggest hidden financial holes in many people's budgets are car expenses. I can almost hear you sighing in frustration as you mutter, "I'm not giving up my car, no matter what this guy says."

I realize that a functioning automobile is a practical necessity for most people today; however, if you insist on always driving a brand new car so you can display a millionaire façade, it is almost impossible to build your millionaire vehicle which will get you to your destination so you can buy any and every car you want.

I live in Oklahoma, and Will Rogers is probably our most famous native son. Although many of his quotes and statements are over a century old, they seem relevant today.

In the depth of the Great Depression, Will Rogers said, "America will go down in history as the only people to go to the poor house in an automobile."

Cars represent the greatest expenditure most people make for things that go down in value. You may have heard the famous truck commercial that features the Bob Seger song "Like a Rock." While the company is trying to promote how tough and sturdy their trucks are, I think about all the people borrowing money to buy new trucks that are instantly sinking in value "Like a Rock."

When I recommend people save money on vehicles that can be reallocated to their millionaire nest egg, I often hear individuals whining, "Well, I have to have reliable, dependable, and presentable transportation."

I'm a firm believer that reliable, dependable, and presentable transportation can be acquired readily within the $5,000 to $10,000 range. Everything over that amount is style and image. I am not opposed to you having style and image unless that spending on the automotive hat keeps you from having real cattle and all the cars you want in the future.

I am not advocating that while you are moving toward your millionaire destination that you live poorly. I am advocating that you live prudently. This prudent spending often comes in counterintuitive ways.

As I shared with you in an earlier chapter, Crystal and I reached that fateful and joyous day when we retired The Green Dog and bought our first Mercedes. That Mercedes was not new. In fact, it was actually 10 years old when we bought it, making it slightly older than The Green Dog.

We drove that Mercedes for 10 more years until we traded it in for another Mercedes. During those 10 years that we drove our first Mercedes, it went down very little in value so that when we traded it in, we were able to get almost all we had paid for it toward our next Mercedes.

When you calculate the true cost of owning and operating that car over those 10 years, you will realize that we weren't living poorly, but we were living prudently. That car gave us safe, reliable, and presentable transportation for a decade; and the day we traded it in, we could have picked you up at the airport in that car, and you would have been impressed with our Mercedes.

Living poorly involves the futile attempt to convince others you've got what you don't really have. Living prudently involves allocating your resources so you can have the things you really want.

Traveling in style does not mean traveling expensively. People today seem to know the cost of everything and the value of nothing. When you evaluate assets based on the joy they bring to you and others instead of how much they cost you so you can impress others, you will begin to have millionaire breakthroughs in your life.

Most millionaires understand the financial trap represented by automobiles. This is why 50 percent of millionaires have never owned a new car and probably never will. The average age of cars driven by millionaires is two years old. These millionaires don't drive two-year-old cars for any other reason than it fits their own millionaire lifestyle and priorities.

Many millionaires own and invest in collections of cars because this is their choice. Remember, it's not about the things you have. It's about the choices you have.

As you are creating a budget or spending plan that will allow you to accumulate seeds to plant toward your financial nest egg, it is important to apply these same principles to businesses you may own or your entrepreneurial ventures.

I remember taking over a company several years ago after their founder and president called me to say, "We would like to meet with you to see if you would be interested in buying us out. Otherwise, we are broke and will be out of business by the end of the month."

Desperation is horrible when you're forced to sell, but it's a wonderful way to buy. When I visited the company in question and met with their president and CEO, I realized that, like most non-millionaire people, this company had wonderful income and great potential but everyone simply refused to control their spending.

As I sat across the desk from this gentleman, I couldn't help but notice the size, scope, and quality of his office furniture. I mentioned his impressive desk, and he proudly told me that they had spent $14,000 on it. In his industry, clients or prospects never came to the office since their business was done over the phone and Internet, so having a $14,000 desk while going broke seemed absurd to me.

When the dust settled, I became the owner of that operation for pennies on the dollar. We did, indeed, have a slight cash flow hurdle at the end of the month, but after I adjusted all of the financial income and expenditures, it took less than $10,000 to overcome the financial crisis at the end of that first month.

As we got over that first financial hurdle and moved ahead toward success, I sat at the former president's desk and considered that he had lost all his hopes and dreams over a $10,000 problem that he couldn't resolve while sitting at a $14,000 desk.

Everybody wants to be a millionaire and many begin to move in that direction, but the vast majority never arrive at their destination—not because they don't have what it takes but because they don't manage and budget what they have.

CHAPTER TEN

Fueling Your Millionaire Vehicle

As you travel the route toward your millionaire destination, you must conserve and manage your fuel.

THUS FAR, WE HAVE EXPLORED the offensive and defensive aspects of your money—offense being the creation of wealth and defense being the preservation of your assets.

Once you have earned money through your employment, entrepreneurial ventures, self-employed efforts, or your own business enterprise, and then you have budgeted your funds as effectively and efficiently as possible, you should be left with a considerable amount of money. This represents the beginning of your nest egg that will become the basis for your total wealth and millionaire lifestyle.

Playing good offense and good defense will give you resources to invest that will grow, multiply, and compound for your future. Please remember, creating long-term wealth is like balancing a three-legged stool. The three legs are offense, defense, and investments, and you cannot win financially by playing well in only one or even two of these arenas.

You've got to succeed at all three in order to reach your millionaire destination.

I began learning about investments and managing money as I was training to be an investment broker for a New York Stock Exchange member firm. I remember, month after month, laboriously slogging through financial texts and test-review material, getting ready for my licensing exam. This is a difficult test for anyone, but for a guy with no formal education in business or finance who was rapidly losing his sight and unable to read, it was a monumental task.

I remember my excitement after I passed the exam and opened my own office, ready to change the world as a 24-year-old through my investing prowess.

My first client who walked in the door was named Mr. Jennings. Mr. Jennings was a legend in the small community where my investment office was located. Everyone seemed to know him and like him, but no one seemed to be quite sure what he did for a living.

He came into my office, introduced himself, and began asking questions. I didn't realize until later he was giving me a job interview of sorts as he cross-examined me, exploring the possibility of us working together. Mr. Jennings was 50 years older than me and had been investing since he was younger than I was at the time, so I found his depth and breadth of real-life experience rather fascinating.

Finally, I guess he was satisfied, and Mr. Jennings became my first client. It wasn't until years later that I understood what truly motivated him to do business with me. After we had experienced years of a successful investing relationship, out of the blue one day, Mr. Jennings said, "Jim, the first day I met you, I decided you would be perfect for me as a financial advisor and broker because you didn't know anything so you wouldn't be forced to relearn it all."

You can imagine my dismay in discovering that all of my hard work in learning and training had meant nothing more to Mr. Jennings than the fact that I was a blank slate for him to begin working with when we began our relationship.

As I look back upon the experience today, a quarter of a century in my life's rear-view mirror, I am grateful for all the clients I had and everything they taught me.

As you contemplate your own investing future, you've got to realize that, while making good returns and establishing growth in your portfolio is important, it is critical that you avoid pitfalls, scams, frauds, and financial instruments designed to enrich everyone involved in the transaction except you.

In an earlier chapter, I quoted one of my heroes, Will Rogers, regarding automobiles. At this point, I think it is instructive for us to review his thoughts on investing.

Will Rogers said, "I am much more concerned about the return *of* my money than the return *on* my money."

As we have discussed earlier, virtually everyone makes enough money to become a millionaire if they play good defense and invest prudently. Your entrepreneurial efforts and business ventures will generate plenty of fuel to propel your millionaire vehicle to your destination if you don't let all of your fuel leak out of the tank by playing poor defense and if you invest your nest egg wisely and make sure it works as hard for you as you work for it.

As you create offense through your business ventures and begin to accumulate and invest your money, you will need a competent team around you. You may think there are a lot of investment professionals, insurance advisors, accounting personnel, bankers, lawyers, and others who populate this profession, but you have no idea how many people there will be clamoring for your business once you have a little bit of money. A few of these people want to help you and are qualified to do so, but many of them simply want to help themselves. They do not have either the ethics or the expertise that you will need to reach your millionaire destination.

The advice about advisors we explored earlier will serve you well as you are building your own millionaire dream team. Don't take advice from anyone who doesn't have what you want.

After becoming a multimillionaire, I began putting my money in some more exotic and complex investments. When you place money in certain private placements, hedge funds, and other accredited investments, you generate some public records and disclosures. These public records and disclosures are like honey to bees. You will begin receiving daily calls from all manner of self-proclaimed financial geniuses and gurus.

I struggled with getting rid of all these people for years until I got some great advice from another multimillionaire. He simply greets the callers and asks them to provide him with two pieces of information before he begins doing business with them. All he wants is their last year's tax return and a current portfolio summary of their investments.

He explains, "Once I know you are a self-made millionaire like me, and you have demonstrated your ability to make and invest your money, I will let you invest mine."

He told me he gets eight or 10 cold calls each week, much as I do, and he has been utilizing his technique for almost 20 years. During this time, he estimates he has asked as many as 10,000 advisors for a simple tax return and portfolio summary before he begins investing with them. To date, no one has taken him up on his offer.

I have interviewed several millionaires and multimillionaires and a few former millionaires who were victims of the Madoff scandal and similar frauds. There will be many bumps along the road of your millionaire route toward your financial destination, but predators like Bernie Madoff are financial head-on collisions with semi-trucks waiting to happen. You won't survive the crash, so let's make sure you avoid them.

You will need to build a dream team of millionaire advisors, consultants, and professionals who are dedicated to helping you reach your own millionaire destination. You can't succeed without this kind of team, but never forget, they are there to advise and serve you as you drive your millionaire vehicle. Never turn your millionaire vehicle over to anyone else and trust them to drive to your destination.

More likely than not, they will drive to their own destination or steer you into a Madoff-like, head-on collision.

Your main defense from these predators consists of diversification, transparency, and disclosure.

Diversification is simply the financial component of your grandmother's advice to "never put all your eggs in one basket."

I spoke to a lady recently who had lost $8 million with Bernie Madoff. If her portfolio had been worth $50 million, this loss would represent a painful setback but not a total catastrophe. But since the $8 million stolen from her represented virtually all her net worth, it represents a financially-fatal wreck which totaled her millionaire vehicle when she had virtually already reached her destination.

Transparency in financial terms is the concept of being able to understand and follow your investments as they are being placed into the market and beginning to grow.

Bernie Madoff and those who are following in his footsteps don't want you to see what is going on behind the curtain and observe their actions. Rest assured, if someone won't reveal what's going on with your investments, it's never good.

Disclosure is the financial concept of understanding everyone's motives involved in a transaction and getting regular updates on the progress of your money. Bernie Madoff generated monthly statements for his victims, so you've got to make sure that your money is protected and the statements being generated are cross-checked and audited.

The first members of your dream team will be your accountant and your attorney. Once again, we want to employ our rule that we don't take advice from anyone who doesn't have what we want. You need to interview prospective professionals in these areas and make sure they "walk the talk." If they are not prepared to verify their own financial success and provide references from millionaires whom they have served, don't walk—run—from their offices.

After you have assembled the legal and accounting portion of your team, you next want to find a good banker, broker, and insurance professional.

Bankers, to a great extent, offer the same or similar services so you want to find one that truly wants your business. You should be dealing with an officer of the bank, at least as you are formulating the relationship, and they should offer the specialized or customized services you will need, not only for your business and entrepreneurial ventures but for your investment matters as well.

Investment brokers and insurance professionals offer the greatest areas of risk and reward among the members of your financial dream team. People who handle investments and insurance are predominantly paid based on sales and not results. It is very important to make sure these people are millionaires and have experience serving millionaires. They should be ready, willing, and able to provide proof and references to this end.

Please understand, there is nothing wrong with any members of your team making money through serving you. Each of the members of my financial dream team are well paid, and I look forward to them making much more money in years to come.

As you develop business ventures and entrepreneurial projects and as you are building your net worth, there will be need for even more professionals and specialized people on your dream team. You may need a financial planner, an estate planner, a risk management consultant, and any number of other specialties; however, in the beginning, your accountant, lawyer, banker, broker, and insurance professional can get you well along the way to your destination.

These people should know and understand your millionaire map and the goals you have planned for your future. They should all be working together in a coordinated fashion to help you reach your millionaire destination.

Never invest any money, undertake any project, or introduce any new strategy to your millionaire map without your own dream team being fully informed and in total agreement.

My investment broker has been a part of my financial dream team for 15 years. I began my financial relationship with him by opening two individual retirement accounts totaling $4,000. Fifteen years later, he helps me to manage and invest more than $10 million in my brokerage account, in addition to my retirement fund and my company's 401K.

My broker knows that my background includes being an investment broker myself. He has spent a considerable amount of time understanding my risk tolerances and return expectations. More importantly, he understands my financial goals and the millionaire milestones between here and there.

If you lose weight, fix up your lawn and landscape, buy a new car, or receive an industry or civic award, people are going to know. Either they can see the difference or they can read about it in the newspaper. The millionaire milestones along the route to your financial goals are not so obvious and, therefore, you won't so readily receive recognition, accolades, and praise.

Your financial goals and millionaire destination may be among your most important objectives in your life. Money is not a vital element of success or well-being for you or your family, but money affects everything that is important to you and your family.

My financial broker knew that I had a goal to get my balance in the brokerage account that he helps me to manage through his firm to $10 million. There's nothing magic or sacred about the $10 million goal. It was simply a milestone to me in much the same way that lifting 400 or 500 pounds was a milestone when I was a weightlifter. Lifting that last pound or compiling that last dollar doesn't make a big difference by itself, but it can make all the difference in the form of a goal or millionaire milestone.

I get up very early in the morning, rising at 4:00 a.m. each day. I can hear your groan of pain and disgust at this point, but realize I am passionate about my work and my life. I don't have to set an alarm at 4:00 a.m. I simply get up at that hour, filled with anticipation, and begin my reading, study, and planning for the day. My investment broker has similar habits, so we talk on the phone most mornings between 4:00 and 5:00 a.m.

I remember the morning I called him and he did not answer the phone using his name, the name of the firm, or even by saying, "Hello." He simply blurted, "Are you dressed?"

I informed him I was still in my bathrobe, and he commanded, "Get dressed, and I will be there in four minutes."

My broker's office is only a few blocks from my home, so I dressed quickly and met him at the front door. He rushed into my living room, shook my hand, and handed me a piece of paper as he said, "I believe milestones should be celebrated."

What he handed me was that morning's printout of the current value of my financial investments in the brokerage account with his firm. For the first time, other than in my dreams and goals, it read over $10 million.

People win who are a part of a great team. Great teams are made up of individuals who understand one another's goals, objectives, and dreams. My investment broker knew about my long-term goal, my millionaire milestone, and the importance of celebrating that victory with me. When you can find these kinds of kindred spirits, it's only a matter of time until you reach your millionaire destination.

Building your investment portfolio is much like designing and making a custom-made suit for you. The tailor working on your suit will need to understand your preferences, your style, your objective, and the milestones throughout the process.

Only invest in things that you know and understand. The self-proclaimed cable TV gurus and experts would have told you in the 1990s that it was impossible to succeed financially without investing in computer and tech stocks. While we have all seen a tremendous rise in the value of Silicon Valley stocks in our lifetime, Warren Buffett avoided investing in virtually that entire segment of the economy because, as he said, "I don't understand it. I do understand Coke and Fruit of the Loom, so that's where I put my money."

No one could begin to argue that Warren Buffett wasn't successful.

As we discussed in an earlier chapter, there are no good or bad businesses or entrepreneurial ventures. It depends on your own talent, time, and temperament. In much the same way, most investments can be appropriate for the right person, at the right time, and within the right phase of their journey represented by their millionaire map.

Always remember that you can succeed in becoming a millionaire by earning money through serving others, playing great defense, by regulating your spending, and investing in things you know and understand. Over virtually any reasonable period of time in the 20th or 21st century, you could have reached your millionaire destination by investing in average-performing mutual funds, quality bonds, and other basic investment vehicles. Anything that seems too good to be true probably is too good to be true.

Remember, you only need to get the bat on the ball and get to first base. Home runs will invariably come from time to time, but they're not your bread and butter. When I look at building my own portfolio from that initial investment of $4,000 to over $10 million, the average return on the average dollar invested throughout the years has been about the overall market return available to every mutual fund or index investor.

I know many self-made millionaires and multimillionaires who have never invested in anything other than bank certificates of deposit. While I don't recommend this as an investment strategy on the grounds of diversification, it is important to note that the return is sufficient.

As you earn and invest your first $1 million and become a millionaire, most of the money which will make up your first million dollars will be money you earned yourself. As your funds grow and you obtain more millions, increasingly, the total will be represented by money that has been earned by your money and not by your own hard work.

Remember, we want to get your money working for you as hard as you worked for it. You can only have money working for you if you earn it by creating value in the lives of others, defend it by managing your expenses and not eating your seed corn, and then investing it prudently in things you and your dream team understand and agree upon.

Prudence in investing is like a speed limit on the route to your millionaire destination. This is not to keep you from arriving at your destination, but instead, limiting your risk will keep you from the fatal crashes that will stop you from reaching your millionaire destination at all.

When you understand that applying each of the principles in this book to your own millionaire map will, inevitably and inescapably, guarantee that you will reach your millionaire destination, you will feel comfortable traveling in safety and security utilizing the cruise control on your millionaire vehicle.

CHAPTER ELEVEN

Taking Others on your Millionaire Journey

As you approach your millionaire destination, you should help others along their route and leave a legacy for future travelers.

NO JOURNEY WORTH TAKING EVER begins or ends alone. It always includes the people we care about.

When you become a millionaire and reach your one millionth dollar of net worth, that single dollar bill should come with a warning label similar to the surgeon general's warning on packages of cigarettes. This million dollar warning might say, "It has been proven that great wealth, given randomly to people who didn't earn it, can be detrimental to their health and future success."

Once you become a millionaire and begin living your new millionaire lifestyle, you will have the understandable urge to help your loved ones and others around you. Your first concern in offering financial assistance to anyone should be the same initial concerns that physicians have when they are confronted with an injured or sick patient. "Do no harm."

There is something that comes from the effort, focus, and energy that it takes to become a millionaire that enables you to live your life of wealth without letting the money ruin your judgment and perspective. People who are instantly given great wealth that they did not earn are often ruined by it.

A study of first-generation millionaires who gave significant financial resources to their children and grandchildren actually showed conclusively that not only the millionaires' net worth was diminished when they made the gift to their children or grandchildren, but ironically, the second and third generation receivers of this unearned wealth actually performed worse financially than their counterparts who were never given gifts of unearned money.

As we explored in an earlier chapter, money and wealth are the result of creating value in the lives of others. If we are given money and wealth when we have not created value, we do not have the perspective and the judgment necessary to manage the money.

It has been estimated that in the near future, $41 trillion in net worth will be transferred from the Greatest Generation, who earned their wealth as we have described throughout this book, to the Baby Boomer generation and to their children known as the Boomer Echo generation. This $41 trillion transfer of wealth represents great potential and great danger.

Among the saddest tasks I ever had to perform as an investment broker was turning over the wealth of my recently-deceased clients to their unprepared children and grandchildren. Never pass along your valuables unless you have passed along your values.

As we discussed in an earlier chapter, when you begin your millionaire journey, you want to get all those loved ones around you on board so they will understand and become involved with your progression toward your millionaire destination. Children are very adaptable and impressionable. You can turn them into responsible, prudent, potential millionaires as you undergo your own journey, but if you leave them in the dark and expect them to come to an instant understanding of the management of wealth, you have created an accident waiting to happen.

In several of my books and movies, I have made the fictitious heroes, who are dispensing wisdom throughout the story, very wealthy individuals. The reason I made Red Stevens in *The Ultimate Gift* series of books and movies a billionaire was to deal with what I call The Big Lie, which is that myth we explored in a previous chapter that wealthy people somehow have wisdom, talent, and expertise that the rest of us don't have.

The wisdom that Red Stevens and other characters in my novels have passed along is wisdom that everyone should leave as a legacy to their descendants. Recent surveys show that 74 percent of the Greatest Generation and 86 percent of Baby Boomers feel that the most important assets they will leave to their children and grandchildren are their memories and family legacies, including the lessons and principles they have learned. This is even more critical if you are a millionaire leaving a significant inheritance to your children and grandchildren.

Maturity is the process of learning from your own mistakes as well as the mistakes of others. Mistakes create pain and difficulty in our lives which cause us to learn lessons of what we want to do or not do next time. Instant wealth can insulate a person from these life lessons. To the recipient of immediate unearned wealth, mistakes don't necessarily create wisdom or maturity. Mistakes just create a mess that some of the unearned money can clean up.

I remember as an investment broker giving tremendous amounts of money to children or grandchildren of my clients who had earned wealth throughout a life of hard work and diligence. These young, instant millionaires had achieved wealth through someone else's efforts; therefore, they had reached a millionaire destination without the benefits of the journey. Unfortunately, in most cases, they frivolously spent all of the money in a few short years or even months, and in many cases, wrecked their health and their future in the process.

We've all read stories about the plight of lottery winners who, after winning vast sums, inevitably file bankruptcy at a rate several multiples higher than the national average. Money does not make you wealthy long-term because money is not the key to wealth. Knowledge is the key to wealth.

If we took all the money in our society and divided it up equally, in a short period of time, it would find its way back to the people who have the wealth now.

Some self-made millionaires just want to give their children or grandchildren a boost. This is understandable and laudable if done appropriately. For the most part, any educational expenses you can provide statistically will result in success for future generations of your family. College tuition assistance, help with the cost of travel for unique study opportunities, and even paying for graduate school may be advisable; however, always remember, people value what they earn, and often a casual gift of college tuition may result in a four-year party for your children or grandchildren.

When I was in college, I spent a year as a dorm leader for 660 young men. Logic might tell you that students who don't have to work for their tuition nor worry about money would have more time to study and take full advantage of their classes. On the other hand, it might seem that students who are working their way through school, holding down one or more part-time jobs, might not perform as well academically as they are faced with so many pressures involving time and money.

My year as a leader in the dormitory observing hundreds of students proved the opposite to me. Young people who worked and earned funds for their tuition studied more and did better in their classes. Young people who were given tuition, expenses, cars, and other gifts from parents or grandparents did not perform as well academically, socially, or in any other pursuit on campus.

My own unscientific study of the hundreds of young men in my dormitory regarding gifts of automobiles may be instructive. I found that young men who were given brand new cars by well-meaning parents or grandparents did not take care of their car or service it properly.

Young men who worked their way through school invariably had older cars but maintained them better, keeping them clean and in good working condition; therefore, while paying for a college education and associated expenses may be a prudent helping hand, avoid making it a handout and think about requiring your children or grandchildren to earn part of the money necessary for their education. You will find them to be more responsible, and they will value the experience to a greater degree. Additionally, you and your children or grandchildren will find out that not all the education during the college years takes place in the classroom.

One practice of millionaires with respect to intergenerational transfers of wealth involves paying hefty down payments for houses that their children or grandchildren would otherwise not be able to afford. Ironically, the statistics show that this will not increase the long-term wealth of your children or grandchildren and will actually contribute to more financial strain and anxiety in their lives.

When you give someone a down payment for a house they otherwise couldn't afford, they immediately are confronted with higher taxes, higher utility bills, more space to furnish, wealthier neighbors to keep up with, and other financial burdens placed upon their family. In the long run, I believe the best thing you can do for your children and grandchildren as a part of your millionaire journey and lifestyle is to teach them how to begin their own millionaire journey toward a millionaire destination of their own choosing.

As stated earlier, money is not the key to wealth. Knowledge is the key to wealth. If you give your children money, they will spend it all without the ability to replenish it; however, if you give them knowledge, they can generate their own financial goals and build themselves a vehicle to reach their own millionaire destination.

If we were to apply the ancient wisdom, "Don't give your children or grandchildren a financial fish, but instead, teach them to fish financially," your legacy of wealth will last for countless generations. The statistics on the net worth of second and third generations who have inherited their wealth are very sad. They are inevitably given money without the requisite wisdom to manage it.

I have the privilege of working with many families of wealth to help them train their second and third generations. It is a process of allowing them to transition from their financial tricycle to the monetary bicycle before they drive the millionaire car. If you just toss your children and grandchildren the keys to a high-powered financial sports car when they haven't mastered the lessons to be learned from their monetary tricycle, you are creating hardships and potential tragedies.

A portion of every dollar you earn must be spent for your current lifestyle, a portion should be saved and invested within your emergency fund and nest egg, and a portion of every dollar should be given away. Giving money to other people and important causes not only improves them, but it will improve you. This is an important element during every phase of your millionaire journey.

Statistically, millionaires give away a higher percentage
of their net worth and income than the rest of society. I
already hear the skeptics whining, "If I had as much money
as a millionaire, I'd be a big giver, too."

In reality, these millionaire statistics are made up of people
who were givers when they were poor and have continued the habit after reaching their millionaire destination.
I would maintain that millionaires don't give because they
have money, but in part, they have money because they
give. Being a generous person is a healthy indicator that
you have an appropriate perspective on wealth and money.

Ebenezer Scrooge was a fictitious character born in the fer-
tile mind of Charles Dickens. While there may be a few
wealthy people who care more about their money than the
important priorities of life, I believe you'll find as you travel
your millionaire journey and meet more people of wealth
that, for the most part, millionaires are generous, caring
people who want to make their life and the world around
them better.

The origin of the word "philanthropy" comes from the
Greek phrase meaning "loving people." In recent generations, its definition has expanded to include simply giving
money. I believe if you are handling the giving portion of
your millionaire journey properly, you will consider philanthropy in the original Greek terms which will involve
loving people. To this end, you will need to understand
how your gifts affect them, both now and in the future.
As we discussed earlier in this chapter, throwing money at
people who are not ready to handle it is certainly not a way
to show your love for them.

Bill Gates, one of the greatest examples of a self-made millionaire in our world today, has often said, "It's harder to give the money away responsibly than it was to earn the money in the first place." Bill Gates and his wife, Melinda, through their worldwide foundation, have dedicated their efforts to giving away unprecedented amounts of money and doing it in the right way.

You should be as practical and purposeful when you give away your money as you were when you earned it. In a recent survey, the number one reason people stated for why they gave their money to the causes and charities they did was simply because someone contacted them and asked for a donation. This is a terrible reason to give your money to anyone.

The representative of the group or organization asking for your donation may or may not work for the most beneficial place for your philanthropy. Your giving should be a result of thought, preparation, and planning. You shouldn't give to someone just because they ask any more than you should buy from someone just because they want to sell you something.

In recent years, a trend has developed among millionaires that is called social entrepreneurship. Social entrepreneurs are people who have succeeded in business or investing and now are turning their considerable talents and energy toward philanthropy. They not only write checks to charities, but they get involved in the management of the organizations and the grassroots tasks performed by nonprofit organizations. Social entrepreneurs want to add a bit of themselves to their money in order to supercharge their gift.

As a speaker, writer, movie producer, columnist, and television executive, I like to add my skills and talent to my money to multiply my impact toward organizations where I give and the people they serve. As a high-priced platform speaker, I have maintained the policy for several years to do one free speech for charity for every event where I get paid. I also do fund-raiser book signings and allow my movies to be used for charitable screenings. With my first movie *The Ultimate Gift*, I was grateful when 20th Century Fox agreed to let us use the movie for over 300 charitable premieres before the film was released in theatres nationally. I was pleased and humbled when these charitable events raised in excess of $20 million for local causes.

Regardless of your profession or business, you can find a way to use your skills and talents, combined with your money, to make a difference in the world.

My late, great friend and colleague, Brian Klemmer, created an event held several times each year that teaches people from around the world how to become a Compassionate Samurai. I have been the opening speaker for each of these week-long events for more than a decade.

The concept of becoming a Compassionate Samurai begins with the premise that there are two kinds of people in the world: those who have power and those who have compassion.

Compassionate people with little wealth or power can't accomplish much on their own. Wealthy people of power are limited in the good they can do until they begin to understand the art and science of acting compassionately.

This book is about living your life on purpose, the same way you will build your wealth, invest your money, and pass it on to others. Your life as a giver must be lived with the same kind of purpose and targeted effort.

Lest you think that becoming a philanthropist is just one more thing to do in your overworked, overstressed life, please understand that giving is the most fun you will ever have with money. If you don't believe this, give yourself a treat and take a group of low-income kids on a shopping spree to a toy store. Their excitement and joy will only be exceeded by your own.

My giving has taken the form of hundreds of college scholarships, a building on a university campus, feeding people around the world, buying air conditioners for elderly people, assisting blind and disabled individuals, promoting literacy in schools, and allowing other charities and philanthropic causes to use my books and movies for their humanitarian efforts. Please remember that my entrepreneurial ventures include developing and distributing movies and television programs accessible for 13 million blind and visually-impaired Americans and millions more around the world.

Your good work need not be limited to charity. As we learned earlier, you can only profit by creating true and lasting value in the lives of others. When you can combine your philanthropic efforts with your entrepreneurial ventures, you become a world changer.

As stated earlier in this chapter, simply giving money to people who don't know how to handle or manage it is not a charitable or truly generous act. You must look at your philanthropy in the same way.

After the tragic earthquake in Haiti, our foundation provided 10,000 meals that were rushed to the docks in Houston to be delivered to starving Haitians immediately following the tragedy. After the initial crisis was addressed and the cleanup and rebuilding in Haiti was underway, the charitable organization that my foundation had partnered with for the delivery of the meals contacted us about supporting their ongoing efforts to feed people in Haiti. I had a lengthy meeting with the leaders of the organization and inquired about their long-term strategy for what I call sustainability.

I like to look upon my charitable gifts as a seed in much the same way I look at my nest egg being applied to my entrepreneurial ventures. This particular organization told me that they had been feeding hungry people in Haiti for many decades and were committed to that work permanently.

While feeding starving people today is the highest possible calling, it's not a long-term plan or permanent solution. I told them I was much more interested in a concept where we could feed Haitians today so that Haitians could feed Haitians tomorrow with the lasting goal of Haitians feeding other hungry people in the world permanently.

Just like your investment dollars, be sure that your charitable dollars work as hard for you and those you care about as you worked to get the money in the first place. The lasting legacy of your millionaire lifestyle and destination is not just the things you can do for yourself, but it's a matter of what you can do for others so that they can do for themselves and, in turn, serve generations to come.

CHAPTER TWELVE

Your Millionaire Journey Begins

A millionaire map, vehicle, and destination are useless until you begin traveling.

The ancient proverb tells us that "The journey of a thousand miles begins with one single step." You have reached the place in your millionaire process when it is time to take that first step. Procrastination cannot be a part of your millionaire journey, and it will be among the biggest challenges you will face enroute to your millionaire destination.

My friend and mentor, Dr. Denis Waitley, often warns people about a dangerous place he calls Someday Isle. Someday Isle is a beautiful, tropical paradise where the waves roll gently onto a pristine beach, and the palms sway in a warm breeze. Someday Isle is a wonderful place to dream and contemplate, but nothing ever happens there.

Denis equates Someday Isle to the people who think, talk, and dream about their destination but never start. They procrastinate and lament, "Someday, I'll get started," or "Someday, I'll move toward my goal." But for those poor people—and I mean poor emotionally as well as financially—someday never comes.

For more than a dozen years, I have written a weekly syndicated column that appears in hundreds of newspapers, magazines, and online publications around the world. Each week in my column titled *Winners' Wisdom*, I seek to give people knowledge they can apply and wisdom they can use as they're pursuing their personal and professional goals.

If you would like to receive my column each week, just forward your email address to Jim@JimStovall.com and let me know. Each of the hundreds of *Winners' Wisdom* columns I have written over the years has ended with one simple phrase, *Today's The Day!* This phrase is the key to every message, every instruction, and every bit of wisdom because it doesn't matter how accurate your millionaire map may be or how enticing your destination seems to you, if you don't get started, you will certainly never arrive. As you think about your millionaire goals, dreams, and destination, you've got to ask yourself, "If not now, when?"

I am adamant about this point because I realize if you don't start on your millionaire journey today, you probably never will.

Every knowledgeable and skilled pilot will tell you that there is one critical point on the runway that must be considered and acknowledged during every takeoff. The aircraft can be fully fueled, serviced, checked out, and ready for the journey. The pilot can know his destination and have prepared and filed his flight plan. The tower can give him the "All clear for takeoff" signal, and he can begin rolling down the runway.

As the plane picks up speed, it rapidly approaches the end of the runway. There is a critical point when the pilot has to make a final decision to either take off or shut down the engines and slam on the brakes. At this critical "point of no return," the pilot must fly it or park it. Any indecision at the "point of no return" will result in disaster.

You are at that point this instant in your own millionaire journey.

Several years ago, I discovered a single, solitary question that helps me clarify and resolve what to do in virtually every situation. When confronting a major task or even a mundane duty, I mentally stop and ask myself my million dollar question: "What would I do right now if I were amazing?" The question doesn't presume that I am amazing, it just beckons me to consider, "What would I do right now if I were amazing?" I have come to realize that if I will act as if I were amazing and perform both large and small tasks in that manner, my life results and the things around me will inevitably be amazing.

As you consider your own millionaire destination and contemplate your potential millionaire lifestyle, you must weigh the price of beginning this journey as well as the lifelong price of doing nothing. As you approach your own millionaire "point of no return" at this instant, I want to ask you, "What would you do right now if you were amazing?"

Your future, the future of those you love, the future of causes you care about, and the future of those who will be confronted with your legacy long after you are gone hang in the balance. Please don't miss this opportunity.

Remember, you're not traveling alone. There are tools, resources, information, and events available to you at www.TheMillionaireMap.com. You can reach me when you're facing questions, challenges, or want to celebrate a millionaire milestone via email at Jim@JimStovall.com or by phone at 918-627-1000.

Stay focused on your millionaire destination and lifestyle. Keep your eyes on the prize while your feet are walking out the journey. Be confident in the certainty that your seeds are growing, and the ships you have sent out will return to you loaded down with your millionaire treasure.

People may ridicule your dreams, make fun of your efforts, and criticize your millionaire map. Remember, only 3 percent of the people in the world will join you in living a millionaire lifestyle; therefore, 97 percent of people can't and won't understand you. Don't listen to anyone who doesn't already have what you want.

My millionaire lifestyle has brought me and those I care about many great things and wonderful experiences.

Even as a blind person, I enjoy traveling to exotic locations and wonderful destinations. As someone born and raised in Oklahoma, I have fallen in love with visiting the ocean and spending a lot of quality time on the beach. I love to get up very early in the morning and walk along the shore just at the water's edge where the sand becomes firm and easy to walk on. I can walk for many miles along the beach that way and find my way back because the beach offers a straight, smooth path.

On many of these walks, I think about where I started, my millionaire journey, and the millionaire lifestyle I live today. I also think about my millionaire future, including the places I want to go and the difference I want to make for the people and causes I care about.

I also think about you, your millionaire dreams, and your millionaire destination. I hope you will travel with me, stay in constant contact with me, and join me in living a millionaire lifestyle.

I look forward to your journey, I look forward to your success, and most of all, I look forward to walking with you on the beaches of the world.

About Jim Stovall

Jim Stovall is the president of the Emmy Award-winning Narrative Television Network. He is the author of the bestselling book, *The Ultimate Gift,* which is now a major motion picture starring James Garner and Abigail Breslin. He has authored 20 other books that have been translated into over two dozen languages. He can be reached at Jim@JimStovall.com.